UNDERSTANDING THE
POWER
GOD GIVES US

UNDERSTANDING THE
POWER
GOD GIVES US

WHAT
AGENCY
REALLY
MEANS

JOSEPH FIELDING McCONKIE

DESERET
BOOK

SALT LAKE CITY, UTAH

Library of Congress Cataloging-in-Publication Data
McConkie, Joseph F.
  Understanding the power God gives us : what agency really means / Joseph
Fielding McConkie.
      p.   cm.
  Includes bibliographical references and index.
  ISBN 1-59038-233-1 (alk. paper)
  1. Free will and determinism—Religious aspects—Church of Jesus Christ of
Latter-day Saints   2. Church of Jesus Christ of Latter-day Saints—Doctrines.
I. Title.
  BX8643.F69M33 2004
  233'.7—dc22   2003023882

Printed in the United States of America   72076-7179
Publishers Printing, Salt Lake City, Utah

10   9   8   7   6   5   4   3   2   1

To our Founding Fathers
who in laying the foundation of our country
laid the foundation for
the Restoration

For the power is in them,
wherein they are agents unto themselves.
DOCTRINE & COVENANTS 58:28

CONTENTS

Contents

INTRODUCTION

*Jesus Christ himself being the chief corner stone;
in whom all the building fitly framed together
groweth unto an holy temple in the Lord.*
EPHESIANS 2:20–21

T here is some danger in suggesting that one gospel principle is greater than another, for it is only in the union of all
gospel principles that the house of the Lord is "fitly framed
together" (Ephesians 2:21). No principle is to be left out or
neglected.

Yet, it is equally true that all principles do not bear equal
weight. Agency, Elder Marion G. Romney said, is the "foundation principle" upon which the gospel rests.[1] Without
agency no part of the gospel can exist. As a gift of God it ranks
with life itself, for without it life has no meaning. To merely
move and breathe is not to live. To live is to feel, to love, to

want, to seek, to learn, to own. It is the right of choice, the power to act according to one's conscience. Agency is light and life, meaning and purpose. It is the lifeblood of all that matters.

Thus, the importance of agency in the divine plan cannot be overstated. Without agency "men would be but puppets in the hands of fate," as Elder Marion G. Romney explained. Indeed, "there would be no existence." For this reason, he said, the preservation of agency "is more important than the preservation of life."[2] To support his point he quoted Doctrine and Covenants 93:30: "All truth is independent in that sphere in which God has placed it, to act for itself, as all intelligence also; otherwise there is no existence."

The importance of agency can be measured in the efforts of the prince of darkness to destroy it. Although the battlefields have changed since the question was asked in council long ago, "Whom shall I send?" the great issues have not. All assembled knew the plan of salvation. All knew the importance of their coming to earth to obtain a body. All knew that in this mortal estate they would be subject to both death and sin and that it would be necessary for One to redeem them from their fallen state so that they might be reconciled with their Father. In the light of that understanding, the Father asked of all assembled, "Whom shall I send?" Two responded, saying, "Here am I, send me" (Abraham 3:27). The first to answer was his Beloved Son, who said, "Father, thy will be done, and the glory be thine forever" (Moses 4:2). The second, Satan (or Lucifer, as he was then known), proposed a universal salvation: Not a single soul was to be lost. In exchange he would take both the agency of men and the place of God. The Father said, "I will send the first" (Abraham 3:27). The second "rebelled" (D&C 29:36), and "there was war in heaven" (Revelation 12:7). The devil and his angels—a third part of the host of heaven—were cast out (Isaiah 14:12–15).

So it is that the war over the plan of the Father continues. The transition from one estate to another brings with it no change in principles or issues. The question remains: Will we accept the Father's plan, or join those who war against it? Will we accept his Only Begotten in the flesh as our Savior and Redeemer? Will we so live as to be a force for righteousness, using our agency as a sacred trust, or will we trade it for a mess of pottage? (Genesis 25:33–34). Will we, like Cain, so deceive ourselves that having killed our brother, or whatever is dear to us, we then declare, "I am free"? (Moses 5:33).

The Battle over Freedom and Agency

We battle for freedom and agency both collectively and individually. In our premortal estate we marched with Michael the Archangel in battle against Lucifer and his legions. We did so to preserve agency and defend the plan of salvation. At the same time there can be little doubt that each of us had individual trials and challenges. Surely, Alma is alluding to such challenges when he tells us we had "to choose good or evil" long before the "foundation" of the earth was laid and that it was necessary even then for us to exercise "exceedingly great faith" (Alma 13:3).

It appears that the battle for agency and the freedom necessary to use it have ever been with us. Obviously, little agency exists in a nation that is not free; yet, living in a free nation does not preclude the loss of agency. In fact, for those without discipline, freedom may pose their greatest danger.

Even if our nation is in bondage (or for some other reason our freedom is restricted), it is still for us to govern our own heart and soul. The test of mortality will be graded on how we used the freedom and agency that is ours. As to citizenship in our own nation, few people in earth's history have been accorded the freedom and opportunities that are ours. A brief review of history sharpens our appreciation of the blessings that are ours.

Following the Council of Nicaea (A.D. 325) and Constantine's uniting of church and state, religious liberty died a swift death. The persecuted became the persecutors. The long night of apostate darkness commenced in which only tattered vestiges of agency were to be found. For fourteen hundred years, men and women were forced to hide the feelings of their hearts from public view. To express their thoughts and feelings could bring ostracism, imprisonment, brutal punishment, and often death. Their servitude was such that in the course of time many forgot how to think and dream and hope. Mankind became like a captive animal in a cage kept in darkness.

Yet, with the passage of time came noble souls whose love of light was such that they could not be kept from it. The tombs of the past yielded manuscripts that spoke of more enlightened days, and a thirst for enlightenment was born again in what historians have called the Renaissance, or new birth. In this war with darkness the Bible was freed from its papal prison and placed in the hands of the common man. The effect was like the warmth that brings an end to the winter, and a newness of life began to spring forth throughout Europe. Gutenberg invented movable type, Columbus discovered the New World, and the Reformers unleashed the power of religious liberty.

Not many generations passed away before men with a Bible in one hand and a rifle in the other set out to conquer the New World and plant the seeds of their newfound faith. Soon the stage was set in America for two great wars, victory in each one being necessary for agency in its purity, with all its attendant powers and blessings, to be restored to the earth. The first war was with King George III and the political power of England. The second was over the issue of religious freedom from the king's illegitimate consort, the Anglican church, as well as from other state-sponsored religions, which varied from one colony to another.

Had the debate over the necessary separation of church and state not been won by those advocating their separation, virtually all that had been won in the war for political freedom would have been lost. Further, it would misrepresent history to suppose that the victory was easily won.

The battle for freedom of religion had to be fought in each of the thirteen colonies, though the battles that turned the tide of this war took place in Virginia, where two noble and great men led the way to victory. These men were James Madison and Thomas Jefferson.

Without political and religious freedom, the God-given gift of agency is prisoner to the state. The purity and fulness of the gospel can exist only among a free people, for freedom is the prerequisite of agency and agency is prerequisite for all other gospel principles. Agency is the sacred space, the mountain, upon which the Lord's house must be built. Victory in the War for Independence had to be both spiritual and temporal if there were to be a First Vision. Victory had to include both political and spiritual freedom.

Thomas Paine foretold that sequence of events: "Soon after I had published the pamphlet 'Common Sense,' in America, I saw the exceeding probability that a revolution in the system of government would be followed by a revolution in the system of religion. The adulterous connection of church and state, wherever it has taken place, whether Jewish, Christian or Turkish, had so effectually prohibited by pains and penalties every discussion upon established creeds, and upon first principles of religion, that until the system of government should be changed, those subjects could not be brought fairly and openly before the world; but that whenever this should be done, a revolution in the system of religion would follow. Human inventions and priestcraft would be detected; and man would return to the pure, unmixed and unadulterated belief of one God, and no more."[3]

In November 1820 Thomas Jefferson, author of the Declaration of Independence, stated the matter thus: "If the freedom of religion, guaranteed to us by law *in theory,* can ever rise *in practice* under the overbearing inquisition of public opinion, truth will prevail over fanaticism, and the genuine doctrines of Jesus, so long perverted by his pseudo-priests, will again be restored to their original purity." To this thought he added, "This reformation will advance with the other improvements of the human mind, but too late for me to witness it."[4] Two years later he announced himself "happy in the prospect of a restoration of primitive Christianity," but "I must leave to younger athletes to encounter and lop off the false branches which have been engrafted into it by mythologists of the middle and modern ages."[5] Four years later, on July 4, 1826, Thomas Jefferson died at the age of eighty-three.

Given that we now stand more than two hundred years removed from it, it is easy to forget that the War for Independence was fought for religious liberty no less than for political liberty. Victory over political tyranny would have rung hollow had it not included full liberty of conscience. Historically, Britain had imposed both its political will and its spiritual will on all its subjects, both at home and abroad.

Indeed, freedom and its companion, agency, are the nursing mothers to light and truth. Their escape from the shackles of a false priesthood and false religion is one of the epic stories of earth's history. Were it not for the events that led to both political and religious freedom in this nation, there would have been no Sacred Grove, no Cumorah, no Kirtland, no Nauvoo—no restored gospel.

CHAPTER ONE

AGENCY AND CHOICE

*Ye are free to act for yourselves—to choose the way of
everlasting death or the way of eternal life.*
2 NEPHI 10:23

In the process of growing up, we learn things that our parents, for one reason or another, did not tell us. One of those things in my case dealt with the principle of agency. For some reason they had forgotten to tell me about the right of choice that was supposed to be mine when they told me what they expected me to do.

I do not remember whether it was in church or from my buddies that I learned about the principle called "free agency," which was explained to me as my right to choose what I would and would not do. I do remember, however, trying out this new doctrine on my father. When the next Sunday morning rolled around, I innocently asked, "Dad, do I have agency?"

"Certainly, son," came the answer.

"Then I am going to exercise my agency and stay home from church today," I announced.

"Son," he said, "in this home you have your agency. That means you can choose to go to church willingly or unwillingly, but you are going to church." Then he added, "Now, get your coat on, or you are going to be late."

His response pretty well typified his understanding of the doctrine and how he applied it in all the other things he wanted to have done that I did not care to do. In fact, the question could be asked whether there has ever been a parent who believed the doctrine of agency applies to their own children. Let's consider the matter.

DEFINING AGENCY

Relatively few words in the dictionary have but a single meaning. Like most other words, *agency* can be defined in a variety of ways for a variety of purposes. In the dictionary of Joseph Smith's day, which generally represents the meaning of words as they were used by the Prophet in the revelations of the Restoration, agency is defined as "exerting power" or the "state of being in action." An "agent" is defined as "one entrusted with the business of another," and an attorney or minister is used as an example.[1] Current dictionaries preserve the same meanings used in Joseph Smith's day.

Latter-day Saints generally think of agency as the right of choice. Although agency includes the responsibility to make decisions, the focus of the word *agency* centers on the power of action and is thus broader in its application than simply making choices. The word *choice* is not used in dictionary definitions of *agency*. The *Dictionary of Word Origins* tells us that a whole family of words has descended from the word *agent,* including such words as *act, action, active, actor,* and *actual.*[2]

WE HAVE NO RIGHT TO DO EVIL

Experience suggests that most Latter-day Saints would, if asked, define agency as the right to choose, particularly to choose between good and evil. At least two problems suggest themselves in such a definition. First, it fails to recognize that agency is a sacred trust given to us by God to act righteously; second, it suggests that we have a right to do evil if we so choose. The capacity to do evil and the right to do evil are very different things. No one has ever done anything that was wrong with the approbation of heaven.

Lehi is an important source on this subject. He said, "The

Messiah cometh in the fulness of time, that he may redeem the children of men from the fall. And because that they are redeemed from the fall they have become free forever, knowing good from evil; to act for themselves and not to be acted upon, save it be by the punishment of the law at the great and last day, according to the commandments which God hath given" (2 Nephi 2:26). Here Lehi is telling us that because of the atonement of Christ, we are free to act for ourselves. He does not suggest, however, that the Atonement gives us any "right" to do evil. By implication, Lehi says, were it not for the effects of the Atonement, we would not have agency, or the power of self-action. He states that men "are free to choose liberty and eternal life, through the great Mediator of all men, or to choose captivity and death, according to the captivity and power of the devil; for he seeketh that all men might be miserable like unto himself" (2 Nephi 2:27).

Teaching this same principle, Alma reminds us that is was by partaking of the forbidden fruit that Adam and Eve became "as Gods, knowing good from evil," who could then "act according to their wills and pleasures" (Alma 12:31). Therefore, God taught them the plan of redemption. Having done so, he gave them commandments "that they should not do evil, the penalty thereof being a second death, which was an everlasting death as to things pertaining unto righteousness; for on such the plan of redemption could have no power, for the works of justice could not be destroyed, according to the supreme goodness of God" (Alma 12:32). So it was, Alma said, that "God did call on men, in the name of his Son, (this being the plan of redemption which was laid) saying: If ye will repent and harden not your hearts, then will I have mercy upon you, through mine Only Begotten Son" (Alma 12:33). There is certainly no suggestion here of any right to do evil.

A few questions and their answers help to illustrate this point:

Question: Do I have the right to reject Christ and his gospel?

Answer: No. The penalty for so doing is damnation (Mark 16:16; D&C 49:5; 68:9).

Question: Do I have the right to break gospel covenants?

Answer: No. Doing so may result in your being cursed with "a very sore and grievous curse" (D&C 104:4).

Question: Do I have the right to suspend the use of my agency, doing only that which I am commanded to do?

Answer: No. The Lord said, "He that doeth not anything until he is commanded, and receiveth a commandment with doubtful heart, and keepeth it with slothfulness, the same is damned" (D&C 58:29).

AGENCY AND FREEDOM ARE NOT SYNONYMOUS

That God gave his children the gift of agency at the time of their birth as spirits and again as they commenced life here on earth is without question (Moses 4:3; 6:56). In order that they might exercise that agency, there had to be freedom—which is also a God-given gift. Agency and freedom, however, are not one and the same thing. Agency, which embraces the power of belief, is absolute. No one can take it from us. Freedom, however, is not absolute. We enjoy it in varying degrees at different times in our lives. A host of external conditions determine the extent of our freedom.

Elder Dallin H. Oaks explained that when Potiphar "put Joseph in prison, he restricted Joseph's freedom, but he did not take away his free agency. When Jesus drove the money changers out of the temple, he interfered with their freedom to engage in a particular activity at a particular time in a particular place, but he did not take away their free agency."[3]

Can anyone take our agency from us? The answer is no. On the other hand, we may, through our actions, choose to surrender our agency even to the point where Satan has "all power" over us (Alma 34:35). Elder Spencer W. Kimball taught: "It is true that the great principle of repentance is always available, but for the wicked and rebellious there are serious reservations to this statement. For instance, sin is intensely habit-forming and sometimes moves men to the tragic point of no return. . . . As the transgressor moves deeper and deeper in his sin, and the error is entrenched more deeply and the will to change is weakened, it becomes increasingly near-hopeless, and he skids down and down until either he does not want to climb back or he has lost the power to do so."[4]

AGENCY IS THE POWER TO DO WHAT IS RIGHT

The formation of our nation provides an excellent example of the relationship between agency and freedom. Our nation was formed by free men for the very purpose of protecting and preserving their rights of choice and action. To this end they established laws to which those who sought citizenship in this nation consented to conform. These laws were instituted to constrain and limit certain actions. These limits and constraints in turn create a climate in which other opportunities and privileges are accorded that could not be enjoyed without that the law.

There was no notion on anyone's part that the citizens of this country had the right to disobey its laws. If people had a right to disobey the laws, then there would be no purpose in the laws. Indeed, there would be no laws, and hence no nation, and thus no freedom.

The same principles apply in the kingdom of heaven. We are free to choose whether we want citizenship in that nation or not. We accept the constraint of heaven's laws to obtain the opportunities and blessings that could not exist without those laws. Having chosen citizenship in God's kingdom, it is not then our "right" to do other than obey the laws of that kingdom. If the lawbreaker—suppose him to be a thief, liar, or bully—can argue that it is his God-given right to be a thief, liar, or bully and as such has a rightful place in heaven, then heaven is no longer heaven. Heaven is not so much a place as it is a people. No place could be heaven if the wrong people inhabit it.

The point is that no government, be it in heaven or on earth, grants its citizens the right to break its laws. Without laws it cannot exist. Its laws in turn were enacted to protect the freedom and agency of its citizens. Thus agency, in the context of the gospel, is properly defined as the God-given power to believe and act in truth and righteousness. Revelation declares, "That which is of God is light" (D&C 50:24). Darkness does not come from God, evil does not come from God, nor does the right to participate in the same.

Perhaps we can pull the matter into sharper focus by likening agency to the power of procreation. While giving us the power to procreate, God did not give us the right to misuse this power. Indeed, he will hold us strictly to account for how we use it. So it is with agency.

Teaching the principles here involved, Elder John A. Widtsoe said: "In our preexistent state, in the day of the great council, we made a certain agreement with the Almighty. The Lord proposed a plan. . . . We accepted it. Since the plan is intended for all men, we become parties to the salvation of every person under that plan. We agreed, right then and there, to be not only saviors for ourselves but . . . saviors for the whole human family. We went into a partnership with the Lord. The working out of the plan became then not merely the Father's work, and the Savior's work, but also our work. The least of us, the humblest, is in partnership with the Almighty in achieving the purpose of the eternal plan of salvation.

"That places us in a very responsible attitude towards the human race. By that doctrine, with the Lord at the head, we become saviors on Mount Zion, all committed to the great plan of offering salvation to the untold numbers of spirits. To do this is the Lord's self-imposed duty, this great labor his highest glory. Likewise, it is man's duty, self-imposed, his pleasure and joy, his labor, and ultimately his glory."[5]

In like manner, also teaching this principle, President Joseph Fielding Smith said: "I have heard people say, and members of the Church too, 'I have a right to do as I please.' My answer is: No, you do not. You haven't any right at all to do just as you please. There is only one right that you have, and that is to do just what I read to you: keep the commandments of Jesus Christ. He has a perfect right to tell us so. We have no right to refuse. I do not care who the man is; I do not care where he lives, or what he is—when the gospel of Jesus Christ is presented to him, he has no right to refuse to receive it. He has the privilege. He is not compelled to receive it, because our Father in heaven has given to everyone of us, in the Church and out, the gift of free agency. That free agency gives us the privilege to accept and be loyal to our Lord's commandments, but it has never given us the right to reject them. Every man who rejects the commandments of our Father in heaven is rebellious."[6]

Agency is given to us that we might enjoy life, liberty, and the pursuit of happiness. It is given to us that we might advance from grace to grace and eventually receive a fulness of all that the Father has (D&C 93:19–20). Properly used, agency will exalt us; improperly used, it will damn us.

FREE AGENTS

Consider how the words *agent* and *agency* are commonly used in the realm of our normal experience. Frequently in the sports section of the newspaper we read about a professional athlete who has fulfilled the terms of his contract with a particular team and so has become a "free agent." As a free agent, he can invite other teams to bid for his services. It is the athlete's right to choose the offer that best suits him. Once he has made that choice and signed a contract, however, he is no longer a "free agent" but rather has become an agent for the team he has agreed to become a part of.

Having committed himself to that team, he accepts certain responsibilities. He has a responsibility to attend practice and to abide by team training rules. He can no longer say, "Well, I have my agency, and I don't have to do that." Of course he has to do whatever is required, and in most cases he is compensated very handsomely to do so.

The point here is that a free agent can do what he or she wants; an agent cannot. An agent is committed to a particular purpose. An agent has exhausted his freedom for the agreed-upon compensation.

MORAL AGENTS

We often hear the phrase "free agency" in the Church. Though it has been frequently used in the sermons and writings of the past, it has more recently been suggested to us in general conference that we use "agency" or "moral agency" instead.[7]

Scripture speaks of our being moral agents (D&C 101:78).

A moral agent is someone who is obligated to act morally. To act morally is more than being moral. All infants are moral beings: They simply cannot do things that are wrong. They are not, however, moral agents because they do not have the power to act, or in other words, the power to bring about change. The more mature the child, the greater his or her agency. That is, a child grows up into the power to act for himself, to make his own choices.

Similarly, as we grow in intelligence—meaning light and knowledge—in obedience, and in faith, our agency grows proportionately. To increase in faith and knowledge of spiritual things is at the same time to increase in agency. Thus, God is the perfect example of a moral agent. No one has a greater power to act in a responsible and moral manner than he does.

Salvation can be granted only to moral agents, because they alone have the ability to distinguish between right and wrong and they alone have the capacity to act righteously.

PARENTS AND AGENCY

I have heard a number of parents say, "I hate agency!" They are simply reflecting their concern that their children are now at an age at which bad choices could prove very destructive and those children want to make all their own choices. These same mothers know innately that granting such freedom to their children would be unwise but fear that refusing to do so puts them in opposition to the doctrine of agency. Their ability to parent might be strengthened by a better understanding of the doctrine.

Let us review what is involved. The gift of agency is the child's at birth. It is not reserved for the parents to bestow upon them at the age of twenty-one or at whatever point the parents feel they are sufficiently mature to receive it. The freedom to exercise that gift is another matter. The child earns that freedom gradually as he or she matures. "Accountability does not burst full-bloom upon a child at any given moment in his life. Children become accountable gradually, over a number of years."[8] For instance, they may have some freedom of choice about what they eat at the age of six and measurably more at the age of twelve. As they prove themselves wise in making such choices, the freedom to choose on this matter is expanded. Controlling our children's freedom of choice is simply a matter of responsible parenting.

All other choices accord to the same pattern. Whatever the choice—be it of friends, music, activities, use of time, whatever—the actions of the children give their parents a measure of their maturity and need for discipline or their readiness to receive greater freedom in the use of their agency. Agency is not the right to do as we please but rather the right to do what is right in each given situation. It requires, as we have seen, both knowledge and discipline. Rather than being at odds with the doctrine of agency when they restrict the scope of their children's choices, parents become partners with the doctrine in shifting responsibility for behavior and decisions from themselves to their children as the children prove themselves wise agents.

CHOICES BRING RESPONSIBILITY

President Henry D. Moyle, a counselor to President David O. McKay, explained the principle of agency in a missionary conference I attended years ago. Apparently he had been told that some missionaries in the mission had said that they had their "free agency" and therefore they didn't have to get up at six in the morning unless they wanted to. President Moyle explained that it had been our right to choose whether we served a mission or not, but now, having chosen to serve a mission, we had exhausted our agency on that matter. We now had no right but to get up in the morning and do the other things required of a good missionary.

It is important that we understand this principle. In saying that we had exhausted our agency when we chose to serve a mission, President Moyle meant that we had exhausted our right of choice on that particular matter.

Let me suggest how this principle works in courtship and

marriage. A young man who is unmarried is free to date and court any young woman who will respond to his advances. Once he is married, however, he loses the right to court other women. He has exhausted his right of choice on that matter, and in doing so he has empowered himself as a married man to raise a family and enjoy all the privileges and blessings of family life. The decision to marry means that he no longer has the right to date or court other women. He does not have the right to fall in love with someone else. He does not have the right to do anything except that which strengthens and enhances the covenant he has made with the woman he has married.

Addressing this issue, President Lorenzo Snow said: "Had we not kept what is called our first estate and observed the laws that governed there, you and I would not be here today. We are here because we are worthy to be here, and that arises, to a great extent at least, from the fact that we kept our first estate. I believe that when you and I were in yonder life we made certain covenants with those that had the control that in this life, when we should be permitted to enter it, we would do what we had done in that life—find out the will of God and conform to it."[9]

CONCLUSION

Good choices enhance agency; bad choices diminish it. Elder Richard G. Scott suggested in a BYU devotional speech that each wrong choice we make weakens our ability to make right choices. Conversely, each right choice makes us stronger and better able to continue making good choices.[10] "Agency," stated Elder S. Dilworth Young, "is freedom to chose right against wrong, not a choice between two equal forces."[11]

My experience suggests that the doctrine of agency has often been misunderstood. Its counterfeits are real and plentiful. The common practice is that those seeking to enslave us to some baser appetite parade before us declaring themselves to be our liberators. They can always be found declaring anything that is "virtuous, lovely, or of good report" (Article of Faith 13) to be a form of bondage. They seek to confuse license with liberty and selfishness with that which is self-fulfilling. In the founding of our nation, we find an eloquent response to whose who would "revile against that which is good" (2 Nephi 28:16).

CHAPTER TWO

LIBERTY OR LICENSE?
THE TESTIMONY OF HISTORY

*All individual human rights were granted on the ground
that man is God's creature. That is, freedom was given to
the individual conditionally, in the assumption of
his constant religious responsibility.*
ALEKSANDR I. SOLZHENITSYN

No principle of salvation stands unopposed. Each has its counterfeits, opposites, and perversions. Agency is no exception. If we are to understand the doctrine of agency and lay claim to the blessings that flow from it, we must first free ourselves from all delusions. Chief among them is the idea that agency is merely the right of choice, the right to choose to do good or evil. To possess agency, it is falsely argued, is to possess the God-given freedom or liberty to do whatever we please. Such a notion stands in opposition to the entire plan of salvation for, as holy writ declares, "I the Lord cannot look upon sin with the least degree of allowance" (D&C 1:31; see also Alma 45:16). Of the revelations of heaven, we are told that "there is no unrighteousness in them" (D&C 67:9). As to the kingdom of heaven, we are told that "no unclean thing" can abide there (3 Nephi 27:19).

Perhaps the counterfeit of agency is best illustrated in the relationship between liberty and license. On this matter history is most eloquent, the sum of its testimony being that liberty and license stand not together but rather as opposites to each other. From ancient times it was understood that the lack of self-control was a form of slavery and thus the antithesis of the free life.

No better illustration of the effects of such thought can be found than the spiritual climate in the Americas before the War for Independence. The idea common to the understanding of the settlers in British North America was that freedom was primarily a spiritual condition, to be found only in self-restraint.

SPIRITUAL ROOTS OF THE RESTORATION

The Puritan settlers of colonial Massachusetts believed themselves to be the embodiment of true Christianity. They thought of themselves as a chosen people with a divine calling and believed themselves to be the contemporary children of Israel. As God had saved his ancient covenant people, so he would save them if they, like their ancient counterparts, covenanted to be his people and to be governed by his word. Their faith held that only when liberty and self-restraint were bound together in a sacred union, one that demanded that each be true to the other, could they obtain the approbation of heaven and have dominion over the earth. Harry Stout, a historian, explained the Puritans' thought process this way:

"If presented in the form of a syllogism, the American Puritans' reasoning would go something like this:

"*Major premise:* God's promises of blessing and judgment recorded in Scripture apply to professing peoples as well as to individuals.

"*Minor premise:* New England is a professing people bound in public submission to the Word of God.

"*Conclusion:* Therefore New England is a peculiar people of God."[1]

In a 1645 speech to the Massachusetts legislature that epitomized the Puritan conception of freedom, John Winthrop, the colony's deputy governor, distinguished sharply between "natural" liberty, which he described as the "liberty to evil as well as to good," and "moral liberty," which he also called "civil or federal" liberty. He associated moral liberty with a "covenant between God and man" and the "politic covenants and constitutions" entered into by men. Such liberty, he held, is the "proper end and object of authority and cannot subsist without it; and it is a liberty to that only which is good, just, and honest. This liberty you are to stand for, with the hazard (not only of your goods, but) of your lives, if need be."[2] Such was the liberty, Winthrop held, by which Christ makes us free (see John 8:32).

Winthrop also reasoned that the curious mix of freedom and servitude could be likened to the marriage covenant. He noted that the woman was free to accept or reject the man's proposal of marriage. Having chosen to marry, she was then to be subject to her husband, but her subjection existed only in the way of liberty and not in bondage. "Such is the liberty of the church under the authority of Christ, her king and husband; his yoke is so easy and sweet to her as a bride's ornaments; and if through forwardness or wantonness, etc., she shake it off, . . . she is at no rest in her spirit, until she take it up again."[3]

Giving Winthrop's illustration a Latter-day Saint twist, we would say that the woman was under covenant to her husband in righteousness, and should her husband choose to act outside the bounds of righteousness, she had no responsibility to sustain him. Although there was perhaps no thought in John Winthrop's mind that the doctrines of "moral liberty" and covenant obligations would lead the colonists to break with the mother country, these very doctrines eventually proved foundational to the revolutionary cause.

Thinking of themselves as the children of Israel, the Puritans naturally saw themselves in the role of building a new Jerusalem in the Americas. Thus, they gave the name Salem to their first settlement. In another of his famed speeches, John Winthrop likened his people to a city built upon a hill:

"The Lord will be our God, and delight to dwell among us as his own people, and will command a blessing upon us in all our ways, so that we shall see much more of his wisdom, power, goodness and truth, than formerly we have been acquainted with. We shall find that the God of Israel is among us, when ten of us shall be able to resist a thousand of our enemies: when he shall make us a praise and glory that men shall say of succeeding plantations: 'the Lord make it like that of New England.' For we must consider that we shall be as a city upon a hill: The eyes of all people are upon us, so that if we shall deal falsely with our God in this work we have undertaken, and so cause him to withdraw his present help from us, we shall be made a story and a by-word through the world."[4]

Winthrop then reiterated the covenant ancient Israel made with their God (Deuteronomy 30:1–3) and closed his sermon with a poetic version of Joshua 24:15, challenging the colonists to "choose you this day" whether they would take on this high and holy task or falter at the gates.

THE CONCEPT OF LIBERTY AT THE TIME OF THE REVOLUTIONARY WAR

At the time of its birth and in its early youth, the American nation was devoutly religious. The two most commonly owned books were the Bible and *Pilgrim's Progress*. In New England, where the thirst for independence was greatest, it is estimated that churchgoers listened to about fifteen thousand hours of sermons in a lifetime and the theme most common to those sermons was that liberty could be found and the blessings of heaven obtained only in self-restraint and in honoring community covenants. That these sermons were heard and acted on is a matter of history.

John Adams, in a letter to Thomas Jefferson, observed that "the *general Principles,* on which the Fathers Achieved Independence, were . . . the general Principles of Christianity," in which he said all sects were united.[5] Of the eighty-eight men who signed the Declaration of Independence and the Constitution, it can be shown that eighty-seven professed faith in God.[6]

The doctrine of freedom that thundered from seventeenth- and eighteenth-century pulpits was "freedom from the rule of Satan, sin, and death" and complete "domination by self-interest and the passions."[7] The liberty of that day embraced voluntary submission to divine standards and the greater needs of the community. Writing in 1766, Stephen Johnson argued that "we are planted in this land for God; and all our deliverances are wrought for God"; and "our forefathers left the dear delights of their native country . . . not for worldly wealth or honours, pomps, or pleasures; but for the glorious cause of liberty,"—"the great and everlasting interests of his gospel and kingdom."[8]

An anonymous author writing in 1759 suggested that the greatest contrast the universe afforded was between liberty and licentiousness. In 1776 Samuel West, a man of some erudition, wrote: "To have a liberty to do whatever is fit, reasonable, or good, is the highest degree of freedom that rational beings can possess."[9] The Reverend Dr. Price, whose works were read throughout the colonies, wrote in 1776, "MORAL LIBERTY is the power of following, in all circumstances, our sense of right and wrong; or acting in conformity to our reflecting moral principles, without being controuled by any contrary principles."[10] John Zubly, a Presbyterian minister speaking to the provincial congress of Georgia, stated that "'liberty and law are perfectly consistent; liberty does not consist in living without all restraint,' and that 'a more unhappy situation could not easily be devised'" than one in which it was supposed that everyone had the right to do just as he wanted.[11] James Wilson, who was appointed by President George Washington to the Supreme Court, argued in his lectures on law that "without law, liberty loses its nature and its name, and becomes licentiousness."[12]

During this era, churchgoers expected to be reminded that "'no natural liberty gives men a right to be *libertines,* or renders them *lawless,* for all are under God and nature. In the most *perfect* state of nature, free from all social and domestic obligations . . . [we] are still bound by the laws of reason and everlasting righteousness. . . . There is no such thing in nature, *as a right or privilege to do wrong.*'"[13] Peter Powers, in a sermon given during elections in Vermont in 1778, stated the matter succinctly: "No man has any right, before God, to believe or practice contrary to scripture. And *liberty consists in a freedom to do that which is right.*"[14]

"Thus, spiritual liberty, unlike contemporary senses of liberty," observed scholar Barry Alan Shain, "captures the recognizable essential features of late 18th-century American liberty: voluntary though communally mediated (and potentially coercive) obedience to true ethical standards derived from a divinely ordered cosmos.

"Spiritual liberty provided the template for an understanding of liberty in which 'every freedom which is freedom for something, every freedom which is justified by a reference to something higher than the individual or than man as mere man, necessarily restricts freedom or, which is the same thing, establishes a tenable distinction between freedom and license.'

This distinction between the freedom to act in ways that might be legal though morally unacceptable (defined as license) and the freedom to act in rationally or religiously responsible ways (defined as liberty), although often implied rather than explicit, was the fundamental distinction that Americans, following their ministers' teaching, maintained between liberty and license. It was spiritual liberty writ large."[15]

The dictionaries of the day defined a libertine as one who exceeded liberty's strict limits, having no respect for religion. Today a libertine is considered simply a dissolute or licentious person, the idea of having respect for religion having been lost.

Even among the unchurched there was a sense of devotion that commonly included family prayer, daily reading of scripture, the singing of gospel hymns, and a commitment to common Christian restraints.

THE CORPORATE COVENANT

The idea of liberty, as known to the inhabitants of this country during the seventeenth and eighteenth centuries, centered in high standards of moral restraint in "which one submitted in service to God, country, and family—in that order" by personal choice.[16] Wrote Shain: "The same reformed Protestants who were so insistent on the need for freedom and voluntarism were willing to force godly living on the damned and saved alike. American reformed Protestants believed that they were individually joined to God through a covenant of grace, yet like the ancient Hebrews, they were being judged by God not just personally, but collectively because of their national or public covenant. Thus, throughout the 17th and 18th centuries, they expected temporal reward and punishment (for example, bountiful harvests or plagues) for their collective actions, and in particular for their sins. Corporate control over the behavior of individuals was not effected in order to gain salvation, for most 18th-century Americans more or less accepted that individual behavior had no effect on one's chances for eternal salvation. (This would radically change in the early 19th century with the great expansion of Methodism.) But whether an individual's behavior was pleasing or displeasing to God was understood to have a significant influence on a community's temporal well-being. So throughout the last years of the colonies and the early years of the nation, when Americans were reported by all to be intoxicated by liberty, appropriate moral legislation continued to be enacted and days of fasting and humiliation continued to be proclaimed."[17]

A historical display in the Library of Congress on the origins of our nation included the following quotation: "Congress appointed chaplains to minister to itself and to the armed forces; it sponsored the publication of a Bible; it imposed Christian morality on the armed forces; and it granted public lands to promote Christianity among the Indians. . . . National days of thanksgiving and of 'humiliation, fasting and prayer' [were] proclaimed [by Congress] at least twice a year throughout the war. . . . Congress was guided by 'covenant theology,' a Reformation doctrine especially dear to New England Puritans, which held that God had bound himself in an agreement with a nation and its people, stipulating that they 'should be prosperous or afflicted, according as their general Obedience or Disobedience thereto appears.' Wars and revolutions were, accordingly, considered afflictions, as divine punishments for sin, from which a nation could rescue itself by repentance and reformation."[18]

Illustrating the people's belief in submission to God, the following proclamation by John Adams, second president of the United States, called for a day of national fasting, prayer, and thanksgiving:

"I do hereby recommend accordingly, that Thursday, the 25th day of April next [1800], be observed throughout the United States of America as a day of solemn humiliation, fasting, and prayer; that the citizens on that day abstain as far as may be from their secular occupations, devote the time to the sacred duties of religion in public and in private; that they call to mind our numerous offenses against the Most High God, confess them before Him with the sincerest penitence, implore His pardoning mercy, through the Great Mediator and

Redeemer, for our past transgressions, and that through the grace of His Holy Spirit we may be disposed and enabled to yield a more suitable obedience to His righteous requisitions in time to come; that He would interpose to arrest the progress of that impiety and licentiousness in principle and practice so offensive to Himself and so ruinous to mankind; that He would make us deeply sensible that 'righteousness exalteth a nation, but sin is a reproach to any people'; that He would turn us from our transgressions and turn His displeasure from us; that He would withhold us from unreasonable discontent, from disunion, faction, sedition, and insurrection; that He would preserve our country from the desolating sword; that He would save our cities and towns from a repetition of those awful pestilential visitations under which they have lately suffered so severely, and that the health of our inhabitants generally may be precious in His sight; that He would favor us with fruitful seasons and so bless the labors of the husbandman as that there may be food in abundance for man and beast; that He would prosper our commerce, manufactures, and fisheries, and give success to the people in all their lawful industry and enterprise; that He would smile on our colleges, academies, schools, and seminaries of learning, and make them nurseries of sound science, morals, and religion; that He would bless all magistrates, from the highest to the lowest, give them the true spirit of their station, make them a terror to evil doers and a praise to them that do well; that He would preside over the councils of the nation at this critical period, enlighten them to a just discernment of the public interest, and save them from mistake, division, and discord; that He would make succeed our preparations for defense and bless our armaments by land and by sea; that He would put an end to the effusion of human blood and the accumulation of human misery among the contending nations of the earth by disposing them to justice, to equity, to benevolence, and to peace; and that he would extend the blessings of knowledge, of true liberty, and of pure and undefiled religion throughout the world."[19]

The previous year John Adams had issued a similar proclamation because of his fear that the "godless and socially radical ideas of the French Revolution might have a demoralizing and disastrous influence on the new Republic."[20] That proclamation, too, called for a day of "solemn humiliation, fasting, and prayer" in which Americans both individually and as a nation acknowledged "before God the manifold sins and transgressions" and sought a "sincere repentance."[21]

A Moral and Doctrinal Drift

The fight for freedom out of which this nation was born was one of religious conviction. Indeed, it was a deep and abiding faith that freedom was first and foremost a spiritual blessing and that it could be found only in self-restraint and in the keeping of community covenants. Benjamin Franklin put it well: "Only a virtuous people are capable of freedom."[22] In short, the freedom they sought was the God-given right to do that which is right.

Aleksandr I. Solzhenitsyn, in his acclaimed work "A World Split Apart," observed that "in early democracies, as in American democracy at the time of its birth, all individual human rights were granted on the ground that man is God's creature. That is, *freedom was given to the individual condition-ally, in the assumption of his constant religious responsibility.* Such was the heritage of the preceding one thousand years. Two hundred or even fifty years ago, it would have seemed quite impossible, in America, that an individual be granted bound-less freedom with no purpose, simply for the satisfaction of his whims."[23]

As a second witness of this sentiment, Shain observed that "America was a land shaped by the tenets of reformed-Protestant theology and spiritual or Christian liberty had an important role to play in this formation. For spiritually awak-ened Christians this is the liberty that frees them from absolute servitude to sin and the necessity of adhering to the tenets of Mosaic law. But less expected than its central place in Christian thought is the degree to which Christian liberty shared elements with other, more secular senses of liberty. They too were characterized by an insistence on voluntary acceptance of a life of righteousness. *Spiritual liberty* was Revolutionary-era Americans' most fundamental understanding of liberty—so much so that it set the standard by which other forms of liberty were judged."[24]

Significantly, "'Puritanism provided the moral and religious background of fully 75 percent of the people who declared their independence in 1776.'" Some authorities place this number as high as 90 percent.[25] "Reformed Protestantism's central role in the sustenance of the concept of personal liberty has been recognized by some of its most obdurate opponents. Even David Hume argued that 'the precious spark of liberty had been kindled, and was preserved, by the puritans alone; and it was to this sect, whose principles appear so frivolous and habits so ridiculous, that the English owe the whole freedom of their constitution.'"[26]

By itself the miracle of victory in the War for Independence was not enough to prepare American soil for the seeds of the restored gospel. There yet needed to be a separation of church and state. Civil and ecclesiastical tyranny had shared the same bed from the time that the church, which had long since lost its virtue, was seduced by Constantine. Political and religious powers had reinforced each other in a swelling tide of blood for fourteen hundred years. From that time until the American

Revolution, true religion was an impossibility. Religious liberty was unknown. The creeds of Christendom, like chains forged in the fires of hell, kept the souls of men captive in the dark dungeon of theological mysteries, where they were guarded and abused both by those wearing clerical robes and those carrying the scepter of the state. The breaking of this alliance cannot be separated from the story of the Restoration. Such is the matter to which we now turn.

CHAPTER THREE

POLITICAL AND RELIGIOUS FREEDOM

*The purpose of separation of church and state is to keep forever from
these shores the ceaseless strife that has soaked the soil
of Europe in blood for centuries.*
JAMES MADISON

On July 8, 1776, a bell tolled from the tower of Independence Hall in Philadelphia, summoning its citizens to hear the first public reading of the Declaration of Independence: "When in the course of human events, it becomes necessary for one people to dissolve the political bands which have connected them with another, and to assume among the powers of the earth, the separate and equal station to which the laws of nature and of nature's God entitle them, a decent respect to the opinions of mankind requires that they should declare the cause which impelled them to the separation.

"We hold these truths to be self-evident, that all men are

created equal, that they are endowed by their Creator with certain unalienable Rights, that among these are Life, Liberty and the pursuit of Happiness—That to secure these rights, Governments are instituted among Men, deriving their just powers from the consent of the governed,—That whenever any Form of Government becomes destructive of these ends, it is the Right of the People to alter or to abolish it, and to institute new Government, laying its foundation on such principles and organizing its powers in such form, as to them shall seem most likely to effect their Safety and Happiness."[1]

The tolling of that bell and the words of that inspired declaration were music to the ears of the "strangers and pilgrims" who had sought so long for a place where they could live and believe according to the dictates of their conscience (Hebrews 11:13). Only where the sound of the Liberty Bell can be heard—only where liberty can be proclaimed—can the truths of heaven be heralded. Only in the soil of free nations can the full blessings of the Church and kingdom of God be administered. Truth and liberty are everlasting companions. To enhance the one is to strengthen the other; to take from one is to impoverish the other.

There is no question that the declaration that the Creator had endowed men with unalienable rights made this a religious, not a political, proclamation. And the pledge with which it concluded made it a sacred covenant between its adherents and the God of heaven: "And for the support of this Declaration, with a firm reliance on the protection of divine Providence, we mutually pledge to each other our Lives, our Fortunes and our sacred Honor."[2]

Elder Marion G. Romney, himself a professor of law, observed that "our political institutions have been structured upon the premise that man is a free agent by divine endowment. Upon this premise the Magna Charta was wrung from King John in 1215."[3] In a similar vein, Kenneth D. Wells, co-founder of Freedoms Foundation at Valley Forge, declared: "When the Declaration of Independence was written, our wise forefathers were schooled in the history of man's quest for freedom. They had the Magna Charta of 1215 clearly in mind. They understood it. There are supposed to be nine men who signed that Declaration who knew the Magna Charta by heart. Others knew the soul-stirring words in the leading sentence of the Mayflower Compact: 'In the name of God. Amen.'"[4]

The Liberty Bell, upon which we read the inscription "Proclaim liberty throughout all the land unto all the inhabitants thereof. Leviticus 25:10," was commissioned in 1751 to commemorate the fifty-year anniversary of William Penn's 1701 Charter of Privileges. This charter, the original constitution of Pennsylvania, protected the rights of its citizens, particularly in reference to religious freedom, the rights of Native Americans, and the right of the people to make their own laws. Of interest is that the line in the Bible that immediately precedes the words "proclaim liberty" reads, "And ye shall hallow the fiftieth year." Twenty-five years later the Liberty Bell was rung at the public reading of the Declaration of Independence.

It is one thing for a people to declare themselves free and quite another for them to win that freedom, for there will always be powers and forces that seek to defeat such an endeavor. In this instance, the War for Independence was to last for eight long and difficult years. Yet, in the providence of God, victory came. As Nephi had seen in vision many years before, "The power of God was with them, and also that the wrath of God was upon all those that were gathered together against them to battle. And I, Nephi, beheld that the Gentiles that had gone out of captivity were delivered by the power of God out of the hands of all other nations" (1 Nephi 13:18–19).

DISCIPLINE AND FREEDOM

Arguably, the colonial army's most important victory was won at Valley Forge, where not so much as a single shot was fired. This was the place of the American army's encampment during the winter of 1777–78. General Washington chose to make his winter quarters at the junction of the Schuylkill River and Valley Creek about twenty miles from Philadelphia, where his enemy was comfortably quartered. Casualties were high, as more than two thousand soldiers found a wintry grave. Their greatest enemy was not the British army but cold, starvation, and disease. They had little more than character and determination for a defense.

In choosing Valley Forge, Washington rejected advice to winter in comfortable quarters west of the Schuylkill River at Lancaster, Reading, or Allentown. He believed that soft billets made soft soldiers. History affords us no accounts of any army that endured more by way of privation and suffering than this untrained band of rebels.

Here it was that a Prussian officer known to us as Baron Von Steuben joined Washington's staff. He observed that no European army could have survived under such circumstances. While deploring the colonial soldiers' lack of discipline and training, he was deeply moved by the way they made light of their miseries and by the depth of their devotion to the cause of freedom. He had never seen an army with such a spirit.

Von Steuben drilled the troops and taught them the importance of discipline and order. In doing so he "discovered the difference between the European and American soldier," writes Robert Leckie. He quotes von Steuben as saying, "'The genius of this nation is not the least to be compared with that of the Prussians, Austrians or French. You say to your [European] soldier, "Do this," and he doeth it. But [to an American] I am obligated to say, "This is the reason why you ought to do that," and then he does it.' Unknown to the baron, while he was making soldiers out of free spirits, they were converting a Prussian autocrat to democracy."[5]

In truth it was not at the junction of Schuylkill River and Valley Creek at a place called Valley Forge that the great victory was won. Rather it was at the point where a river called Freedom and another called Discipline began to flow together as one that the army that would eventually secure freedom for themselves, their children, and their children's children was forged.

THE BATTLE FOR RELIGIOUS FREEDOM

So it was that a great nation was formed and a constitution created, both based on the principles of heaven. By the Spirit of revelation, Joseph Smith stated it thus: "That every man may act in doctrine and principle pertaining to futurity, according to the moral agency which I have given unto him, that every man may be accountable for his own sins in the day of judgment. Therefore, it is not right that any man should be in bondage one to another. And for this purpose have I established the Constitution of this land, by the hands of wise men whom I raised up unto this very purpose, and redeemed the land by the shedding of blood" (D&C 101:78–80).

In an earlier revelation the Lord had affirmed his approval of the Constitution: "And now, verily I say unto you concerning the laws of the land, it is my will that my people should observe to do all things whatsoever I command them. And that law of the land which is constitutional, supporting that principle of freedom in maintaining rights and privileges, belongs to all mankind, and is justifiable before me. Therefore, I, the Lord, justify you, and your brethren of my church, in befriending that law which is the constitutional law of the land; and as pertaining to law of man, whatsoever is more or less than this, cometh of evil. I, the Lord God, make you free, therefore ye are free indeed; and the law also maketh you free" (D&C 98:4–8).

Having won their political independence, framed a constitution, and formed a nation, the now-independent Americans found the stage set for the second great war of the Revolution: the fight for religious liberty. The landmark battles in this struggle were fought in Virginia, the new Union's most populous state. Its example carried great weight, and four of the first five presidents of the United States were Virginians. These same men had played significant roles in the Constitutional Convention. The battles for religious liberty involved more than a decade of political wrangling, but it could be no other way. These men had shed their blood for the right to disagree. These disagreements were "the severest contests in which I have ever been engaged,"[6] Jefferson acknowledged.

Victory came slowly as the religious laws fell, one after another. They included laws that had mandated church attendance, proscribed the form one must follow in worship, and made denial of the Trinity an imprisonable offense. Heresy, as defined by the Anglican church, ceased to be a capital offense. To that point Roman Catholics had been precluded from holding public office, and "free thinkers" had been in danger of having their children taken from them. Jefferson led the fight to bring an end to all such practices.[7]

It was in the argument for compromise that religious freedom faced its greatest danger. It was argued that although it was clearly inappropriate to continue to give preferential status to the Church of England, that did not mean that every official tie between religion and society had to be broken. Patrick Henry led the fight for a bill that would make Christianity the state's official religion. Madison was quick to point out the flaw in such a position. He "urged his readers to consider that a bill establishing Christianity to the exclusion of all other religions could at any time 'establish with the same ease any particular sect of Christians, in exclusion of all other sects.'"[8] Had Patrick Henry's eloquence exceeded James

Madison's logic, we could have been right back where we were before Lexington and Concord, Valley Forge and Yorktown.

True religion, Madison argued, could only be propagated by reason and persuasion, never by power, position, or with the sword. There must be, as religious reformer Roger Williams expressed it, "a wall of separation between the garden of the church and the wilderness of the world."[9] The lesson of history, said Madison, was that in all the centuries since Constantine nothing good had come from the disastrous union of church and state. Among the clergy it produced "'more or less in all places, pride and indolence,'" and among the laity, "'ignorance and servility.'" It brought in its wake "'superstition, bigotry, and persecution.'"[10] The gem of the Christian faith had gleamed most brightly, he declared, when the faithful suffered adversity rather than patronage, and religious leaders served most honestly when they depended not upon the state but upon the fruits of their own labors for their livelihood.

It was clear to the memory of these men that "in 17th-century England, bishops wielded enormous political as well as spiritual power. Bishops were officers of the state, members of the powerful House of Lords, agents of persecution and oppression. And much of this bad odor clung to bishops in the 18th century as well."[11] To the minds of Jefferson and Madison, the "Bishops represented ecclesiastical tyranny, bloody persecution, lordly living, and imperious judging."[12] Many of our forefathers had fled England to escape their authority.

Thomas Jefferson asked to be remembered on his tombstone for only two achievements: the writing of the Declaration of Independence and the statute for establishing religious freedom in the state of Virginia. That statute began thus: "Whereas Almighty God hath created the mind free; that all attempts to influence it by temporal punishments or burthens, or by civil incapacitations, tend only to beget habits of hypocrisy and meanness, and are a departure from the plan of the Holy author of our religion, who being Lord both of body and mind, yet chose not to propagate it by coercions on either, as was in his Almighty power to do. . . .

"[And whereas] the impious presumption of legislators and rules, civil as well as ecclesiastical, who being themselves but fallible and uninspired men, have assumed dominion over the faith of others, setting up their own opinions and modes of thinking as the only true and infallible, and as such endeavoring to impose them upon others, hath established and maintained false religions over the greatest part of the world, and through all time. . . .

"[And whereas] truth is great and will prevail if left to herself, that she is the proper and sufficient antagonist to error, and has nothing to fear from the conflict, unless by human interposition disarmed of her natural weapons, free argument and debate, errors ceasing to be dangerous when it is permitted freely to contradict them."[13]

Jefferson's statute underwent considerable revision, but the essence of it survived. Thereby, the doctrine of religious liberty was established in Virginia and a pattern set for the rest of the nation. To our everlasting blessing, that pattern was followed.

A PREPARED PEOPLE

The Lord, having brought a chosen people "out of captivity" to this land and blessed them in obtaining their independence, now gave direction to the events that would make possible the restoration of his gospel (1 Nephi 13:16).

Those events had been foreseen and recorded by prophets who have claim—binding in the courts of heaven—to an everlasting possession of this land. To the ancient fathers of this land, Christ promised that he would gather those of the house of Israel and that he would establish them "in this land, unto the fulfilling of the covenant which I made with your father Jacob; and it [this land] shall be a New Jerusalem" (3 Nephi 20:22). "It is wisdom in the Father," he said, "that they should be established in this land, and be set up as a free people by the power of the Father," that the message of the restored gospel and the covenant of salvation might be taken to "a remnant" of the seed of those faithful inhabitants of this land, "that the covenant of the Father may be fulfilled which he hath covenanted with his people, O house of Israel" (3 Nephi 21:4).

It rather understates the matter to say that the history of the founding of our nation and the early history of our Church are one and the same. Had this nation not been formed, the gospel could not have been restored, for the simple reason that the truths of heaven require freedom to exist as we require air to breathe. Had this nation not been brought into existence, the covenants of the Father to the ancient inhabitants of this land and to the seed of Abraham scattered throughout the world could not be brought to fruition. Indeed, the New Jerusalem would remain un-built, Israel un-gathered, the covenant God made with the ancients un-fulfilled, and the very purpose for which this earth was created left un-accomplished.

A Nation Was Born

The colonial soldier was not fighting for the freedom to be idle. He had no fear of hard work. He fought, rather, for the right to be his own master. He wanted his own piece of land, where his fortune rested on his own sweat and his own ingenuity. He respected the need for community and was willing to help support the same and rightfully expected to have some voice in it. If he was consistent in his reasoning, he heeded the same principles in the realm of spiritual things. That is, he expected to work out his salvation with fear and trembling. He did not curry the favor of heaven in the deceitful hope that he could obtain God's blessing while living at odds with God's standards. He did not expect to reap where he had not sown, nor did he expect to find freedom in anything other than self-restraint. Such were the principles upon which the host nation of the Restoration was founded.

CHAPTER FOUR

PREREQUISITES FOR AGENCY

*For I have sworn upon the altar of God, eternal hostility
against every form of tyranny over the mind of man.*
THOMAS JEFFERSON

Compulsion is the tool of tyrants, the companion of deception, and the sure sign of false religion. By contrast, the freedom to choose who and what one believes and how one will
live and worship is the very essence of God's plan for the salvation of his children. There can be no true religion without
freedom of both thought and action.

Agency, which embraces the right of choice, is bedrock to
all the doctrines of heaven, where only that offering born of free
will is accepted. In the telling of the story of the Grand Council,
it is sometimes said that Lucifer sought to force all men to do
good or to live right. Such a notion finds justification neither in

the scriptural text nor in logic. The only text that bears on the matter quotes Lucifer as saying, "Behold, here am I, send me, I will be thy son, and I will redeem all mankind, that one soul shall not be lost, and surely I will do it; wherefore give me thine honor" (Moses 4:1).

In that expression we find Lucifer promising to redeem, or save, all mankind, but there is no mention of any need to have them live in any particular way. Indeed, if people are forced to do something, the very fact that they have been forced to do it robs the action of any meaning. What meaning could there be in an expression of love given under duress? What meaning is there in the reelection of a tyrant when he runs unopposed on a ballot that has no place for a negative vote and everyone of voting age is forced to vote? What purpose would be served in making a covenant to live a particular standard when there was no choice to do otherwise?

Unless individuals have the right of choice, a just God could neither exalt nor condemn their actions. If Satan could in truth be blamed for all the evil that people do, we would then be faced with the question of whether God could in justice hold us accountable for our actions. In our zeal to assure people that they are loved and to prove that we are both loving and forgiving, it is not uncommon to hear people make expressions to this effect: "We hate the sin but love the sinner." The idea seems to be that somehow we can dissociate the sin from the person who committed it. If this idea really worked, we would excommunicate sins instead of sinners.

Several years ago someone gave one of my young sons a whistle. He immediately commenced to march through the house blowing it as loud as he could. When I explained to him that the noise must stop, he said, "But, Dad, I'm not making the noise. The whistle is." Nevertheless, if discipline were forthcoming, it would have gone to my son, not to the whistle.

What is important here is that we can correct only that behavior for which we are responsible. To improperly deny responsibility for a particular problem is at the same time to remain blind to the opportunity to correct it. Agency, which is the power to bring about change, requires responsible behavior.

Conditions Necessary for the Exercise of Agency

Four conditions are required for the existence of agency. They are, first, that "laws must exist"; second, "opposites must exist"; third, a knowledge of the laws and opposites "must be had by those who are to enjoy the agency"; and fourth, there must be an "unfettered" right of choice.[1] Let us briefly consider each.

Laws Must Exist

Laws are instituted to establish order. Thus, God instituted laws whereby we as his children could lay claim to the blessings of heaven. "For all who will have a blessing at my hands," the Lord said, "shall abide the law which was appointed for that blessing, and the conditions thereof, as were instituted from before the foundation of the world" (D&C 132:5).

Teaching the importance of laws, Lehi reasoned: "If ye shall say there is no law, ye shall also say there is no sin. If ye shall say there is no sin, ye shall also say there is no righteousness. And if there be no righteousness there be no happiness. And if there be no righteousness nor happiness there be no punishment nor misery. And if these things are not there is no God. And if there is no God we are not, neither the earth; for there could have been no creation of things, neither to act nor to be acted upon; wherefore, all things must have vanished away" (2 Nephi 2:13).

It is a common ploy of antichrists to deny that God speaks or that there are absolutes (meaning commandments). The devil trains his agents well. He knows that the victory is his if he can destroy the idea that commandments are to be taken seriously. Between Satan and his agents, there will always be someone to tell you that keeping commandments robs you of your freedom or your agency.

During the Vietnam War, I served in the military as a

chaplain. In that capacity I spent a lot of time counseling with soldiers in the stockade. Most of them were there because they had gone AWOL. When I asked why they had run away, they invariably responded, "Because I wanted to be free." Somehow they had the idea they could obtain freedom by running away from their duty.

I would tell them that I also wanted my freedom, but rather than run away, I had chosen to stay and do my duty. As I left them in the stockade, I invited them to consider who had the greatest freedom: me or them?

Be assured that Satan is at war with all of God's commandments. He or his agents can always be found arguing against the necessity of our keeping commandments or that the consequences associated with breaking them will not really be that great.

To oppose divinely given law is at the same time to oppose the doctrine of agency. A philosophy, for instance, that tells the guilt-ridden that they are carrying an unnecessary burden, that they really have not sinned, and that God loves them irrespective of what they do, leaves them with no way to cleanse themselves from the stench of sin.

Opposites Must Exist

The apostles of the prince of darkness accomplished the same end—that is, negate divine law by denying the existence of opposites. We train teachers to do this. We tell them never to tell students they are wrong for fear that our doing so might intimidate or discourage them. Regardless of how dumb-headed they might be, we tell teachers to accept students' comments with such statements as, "Well, that's an interesting thought," or "I never thought of that before." The sin of sins would be to tell them they were wrong and suggest that a change was in order. Such a course would result in a bad student-teacher evaluation. Too many poor evaluations, and the teacher is out of a job. Further, to tell one student that he is wrong gives the uncomfortable feeling to the rest of his classmates that they, too, might be wrong about something. Heaven forbid! After all, how could learning take place in an environment where a higher standard is held and people are challenged to change?

Thus, the classroom becomes a sanctuary in which there is no right or wrong. What matters is only that everyone be tolerant and nonjudgmental. Here, all students feel secure and safe, knowing that regardless of what they choose to do or not do, their academic salvation is assured. The haunting problem is that this whole scenario sounds dangerously like the philosophy espoused by Satan in the great council of heaven. The difference, it might be said, is that students are not seeking to overthrow teachers, but then, that is hardly necessary in a situation in which teachers have already abdicated their role. Of moment is that in all of this, we have created classrooms in which students cannot empower themselves to act in a positive way. Indeed, there is no positive way because that would suggest that there was a negative way—which suggestion might hurt someone's feelings.

The point is that if there are no laws, no standards, no opposites, and no choices, there can be no agency. By eliminating the possibility of failure, we eliminate the opportunity to succeed.

Knowledge Is Essential

How essential is knowledge to the doctrine of agency? The gospel message has as its purpose bringing us "out of darkness unto light—yea, out of hidden darkness and out of captivity unto freedom" (2 Nephi 3:5).

There is great power in the knowledge of eternal truths. Knowledge of truth expands our power to act. That is why Satan declared war on truth. That is also why apostate religions describe God as incomprehensible and unknowable. That explains why people are forever telling our missionaries that it is not what you believe but how you believe that counts. That is why they sometimes become offended at the idea that there can be only one true and living Church on the face of the whole earth. That is why the agents of the prince of darkness tell us to be open-minded and nonjudgmental.

This is why they are constantly leading so-called liberation movements. Check the fine print. What they would liberate us from is light, and when we lose the light, we also lose our power to act as an agent.

Infant children, though both pure and innocent, are completely helpless. They lay claim to their birthright of agency only as they obtain knowledge. There is no agency in ignorance. We cannot call upon the God of heaven without first knowing that there is one. We cannot disperse the powers of darkness until we know where light is to be found. We cannot exercise faith in principles that are not true. Agency requires knowledge. We cannot act on intelligence that we do not have. A lesser gospel may entitle us to associate with angels, but we can walk with God only after we have obtained the fullness of his gospel.

The light of heaven never goes unopposed. As the prince of darkness attacked the youthful Joseph Smith when he knelt to pray in what we know as the Sacred Grove, so can the prince of darkness be expected to oppose every effort on the part of every soul who seeks that same light. And as Joseph Smith was rescued by the light of heaven from that darkness, so can we expect the same.

Standing opposite the greatest truths known to this world will always be the greatest heresies. We can possess no greater knowledge than the knowledge that God is the Father of our spirits and the Creator and Author of all things. The greatest cloud of darkness known to this mortal sphere is made of the arguments, theories, and philosophies of men and devils that seek to obscure or hide the knowledge of God.

The second greatest body of truths centers in Christ and his role as our Redeemer and Savior. So it is that the second greatest body of darkness and confusion consists of the opposition to or perversion of Christ's role in redeeming us from the effects of the fall of Adam.

The third greatest body of heresy centers in obscuring or denying the place of the Holy Ghost as a revelator and testator. In short, Satan is at war with the light of heaven and always seeks to block it. By obscuring truth he limits the knowledge upon which we could otherwise act as agents.

Unfettered Choice Must Exist

The fourth prerequisite for agency to exist is that of unfettered choice. The thirteen colonies that originally formed our nation consisted of people transplanted from the Old World. These new settlers brought their Bibles, their creeds, their religious traditions, prejudices, and intolerances with them. Though they themselves sought the freedom to worship as they chose, the idea that others should have that same privilege came slowly. Indeed, it came reluctantly, and unevenly. The history of religion and the early churches in America includes its share of intolerance, fines, whips, witch hunts, jails, and gallows. The soil of the New World was seeded with both wheat and tares.

All of this should be no surprise, given the traditions in which the thought patterns of these New World emigrants had been fashioned. In A.D. 325 when Constantine chose to wed the Christian faith to the destiny of Rome—thus making church and state one—the hope of true religion was lost to the Roman Empire. For well over the next thousand years, the history of religion in Europe is the story of the Bible and the sword, as historian Barbara Tuchman entitled her account of that tumultous period. No longer did the Church respond to those who might disagree with her by moral authority, persuasion, and discourse. To disagree with the church became heresy, and in offending the church, one also offended the state. That made treason of heresy. Even silence was sufficient to bring the charge of treason and death by beheading to Sir Thomas More, who had been quick to see that those disagreeing with King Henry's beliefs would be executed. No longer were men endowed with the power of choice in matters of faith. What they were to believe or not believe, as the case may be, was dictated by law, with woeful consequences for those daring to think otherwise.

In his work *A World Lit Only by Fire,* historian William Manchester observed: "Medieval Christians, knowing the other cheek would be bloodied, did not turn it. Death was the prescribed penalty for hundreds of offenses. . . . The threat of capital punishment was even used in religious conversions, and medieval threats were never idle. Charlemagne was a just and enlightened ruler—for the times. His loyalty to the Church was absolute, though he sometimes chose peculiar ways to demonstrate it. Conquering Saxon rebels, he gave them a choice between baptism and immediate execution; when they demurred, he had forty-five hundred of them beheaded in one morning." There was nothing unusual in this, Manchester notes, "Soldiers of Christ swung their swords freely. And the victims were not always pagans."[2] The Arian controversy, which followed Constantine's decision at the Council of Nicaea, resulted in riots in which more Christians were killed by Christians than had died in the Roman persecutions.

"In 1492, the year of Columbus, Spain's Jews were given three months to accept Christian baptism or be banished from the country. . . . Between thirty thousand and sixty thousand were expelled. . . . The king of Portugal, finding merit in the Spanish decree, ordered the expulsion of *all* Portuguese Jews. His soldiers were instructed to massacre those who were slow to leave. During a single night in 1506 nearly four thousand Lisbon Jews were put to the sword."[3]

"In instances in which pilgrims had offended God and

man," Manchester writes, "their journeys were actually a substitute for prison terms. European castles had dungeons—so did the Vatican—but they couldn't begin to hold the miscreant population. The chief legal penalty was execution. There were alternatives in lay courts—ears were cut off, tongues ripped out, eyes gouged from their sockets"—but such actions were not sufficient to balance the scales of justice and no hope of salvation could be extended to the transgressors.[4]

Puritans and Pilgrims came to the New World for the express purpose of getting as far away as possible from the corruption of the Church of England. This set a tone. When the Church of England did arrive in Boston, it did so at the point of the sword. Where England went, the Church of England went also. To plant her flag on new soil was at the same time to transplant her religion, which made civil and ecclesiastical law one.

Roger Williams, commenting on the religious history of England, observed, "It hath been England's sinful shame to fashion and change her garments and religions with wondrous ease and lightness, as a higher power, a stronger sword, hath prevailed; after the ancient pattern of Nebuchadnezzar's bowing the whole world in one most solemn uniformity of worship to his golden image."[5]

Arguing against the illicit union of church and state, Thomas Jefferson reminded his fellow patriots that if an all-wise and all-powerful God restrained himself from coercing either the bodies or the minds of men and women, it was utterly absurd for fallible and uninspired men to assume dominion over the faith of others. State-coerced religion, he said, succeeded only in making "one half the world fools, and the other half hypocrites."[6]

With civil and ecclesiastical tyranny joining hands to enslave the world, only the union of political and religious liberty could emancipate it. Supporting the alliance of church and state was "the force of history," wrote Edwin S. Gaustad, a noted historian. "Against entrenched positions of such potency and hoary respectability, only a mighty counterthrust could hope to nudge a reluctant world away from its bloodied soil of persecution toward a higher ground where all consciences might be free."[7]

"Just as civil and ecclesiastical tyranny had marched side by side through the centuries, each reinforcing the other and thereby swelling the flow of blood, so the battle for liberty could not cease until completed on both political and religious fronts."[8]

Gaustad observed that "in 1793 Priestley published a lengthy work entitled *An History of the Corruptions of Christianity,* an exposé of what early Christian theologians had done to mystify, Hellenize, Platonize, and generally corrupt the pure primitive gospel of Jesus Christ. When Jefferson read and reread this work in the 1790s, he saw new doors of under-standing open wide before him. He thought that he had rejected Christianity; now he realized that it was only the cor-ruptions of Christianity that he had rejected! Those corrup-tions, unfortunately, so pervaded all of Christendom that the genuine article was lost almost beyond rescue."[9] Yet, it was res-cued, and two men who played an important role in that rescue were James Madison and Thomas Jefferson, for both political and religious freedom had to be established for a pure religion to exist.

The United States of America was formed for that purpose. America's greatest contribution to the concept of government is that of religious freedom, meaning the separation of church and state and the voluntary support of religion, thus giving men a choice where matters of faith are concerned. "We are teaching the world," said James Madison, "the great truth that governments do better without kings and nobles than with them. The merit will be doubled by the other lesson that reli-gion flourishes in greater purity, without than with the aid of government."[10]

CHAPTER FIVE

AGENT OR INSTRUMENT?

*If I ask Him [God] to give me wisdom concerning any requirement in life
. . . and get no answer from Him, and then do the very best that
my judgment will teach me, He is bound to own and
honor that transaction, and He will do so.*
BRIGHAM YOUNG

The gospel consists of a host of principles, no one of which
has the power of salvation in it. Salvation is to be found only
in the unity of those principles. None is to be left out, and
none is to be exalted above the others. All must be placed in
proper and perfect balance. The grace of Christ cannot exclude
the necessity of obedience to the laws and ordinances of the
gospel any more than those laws and ordinances can supplant
the role of Christ as our Savior and Redeemer. No gospel principle can stand alone, nor can it dominate other principles.
The command to reprove "with sharpness, when moved
upon by the Holy Ghost" is to be followed by an increased

expression of love (D&C 121:43). The two must be in balance—the gospel embraces more than just love. It includes the necessity of correction. We cannot raise our children on love without discipline or on discipline without love. Both are necessary. A proper balance must exist.

AGENCY AND REVELATION: THE BALANCE

That same God who twice gave each of his children the gift of agency—first as spirits and again as they were born into this mortal sphere—also instituted laws that are irrevocable, laws to which all must submit or lose their divine inheritance. So it is that our right of self-government is to be submissive to the principle of revelation, and yet the principle of revelation is to be submissive to the integrity of our agency. Well might we ask, "What are the principles by which we find and maintain so fine a balance?"

It stands to reason that in granting the gift of agency, God did not intend that each of us re-decide the Ten Commandments or the necessity of repentance and baptism. The principles of salvation are not negotiable, for they are of God's making, not ours. The gift of agency grants to each of us the right to choose whether we will embrace and live these commands. It does not grant us the power or authority to change them. Thus, if God commands that we leave Egypt and go to

Sinai, we do not take up the argument that it would be much wiser for us to go to Mount Nebo. There will, however, be a host of decisions that need to be made to get us and our families from Egypt to Sinai. At issue is whether it is our responsibility or God's to get us to Sinai. If the responsibility rests with God, we may appropriately wait for his direction in all things, never acting independent of divine command. On the other hand, if the responsibility rests with us, we had better get going.

To the early Saints of this dispensation, the Lord said, "For behold, it is not meet that I should command in all things; for he that is compelled in all things, the same is a slothful and not a wise servant; wherefore he receiveth no reward. Verily I say, men should be anxiously engaged in a good cause, and do many things of their own free will, and bring to pass much righteousness; for the power is in them, wherein they are agents unto themselves. And inasmuch as men do good they shall in no wise lose their reward. But he that doeth not anything until he is commanded, and receiveth a commandment with doubtful heart, and keepeth it with slothfulness, the same is damned" (D&C 58:26–29).

It is helpful to have some understanding of God's purpose in taking his people out of Egypt and marching them to Sinai. There are certain blessings to be administered at the Holy Mountain that cannot, in the providence of God, be administered in any other place. There are also experiences to be obtained in making the journey, experiences that we may not be able to obtain in any other way. The difficulty of the journey will harden and season the Lord's people, thinning their ranks so that those whose commitment is weak separate themselves from the ranks of the faithful. Thus, both the journey and the destination are of marked importance.

The grand key to all of this is that God will not do for his people what they can do for themselves. He will sustain them by miracles only as miracles are required. It is not his purpose to spoil and pamper his children. His purpose is to make them strong, wise, and independent. How they are to accomplish the journey rests in large measure with them. They may seek his help and receive it but only after they have exhausted their capacity to act as agents for themselves.

The principles involved have been clearly established for those of our day. The lessons in Oliver Cowdery's experience in translating the Book of Mormon are particularly important. Doctrine and Covenants 8 is essentially a "how to" manual for translation. The Lord told Oliver: "I will tell you in your mind and in your heart by the Holy Ghost, which shall come upon you and which shall dwell in your heart. Now, behold, this is the spirit of revelation; behold, this is the spirit by which Moses brought the children of Israel through the Red Sea on dry ground" (D&C 8:2–3). Oliver was also directed to "doubt not" and to "ask," that he might "know the mysteries of God" and that he might translate (D&C 8:8, 11).

The story of what happened from this point is well known. Oliver commenced to translate, doubted, and stumbled. The Lord explained to Oliver that his preparation and efforts had been insufficient. "You must," the Lord said, "study it out in your mind; then you must ask me if it be right" (D&C 9:8).

The principle we are getting here is our responsibility in the process of receiving revelation. It is not just a matter of our obtaining the mind and will of the Lord. How we get the revelation is important, and the "how" of the matter is that we must first do all within our own capacity before the Lord will take over or before we can expect him to confirm our efforts. We find the same principle operative when John, called the Baptist, came to restore the Aaronic Priesthood. He first conferred the priesthood on Joseph and Oliver and then directed them to baptize each other. Now there is not a reason in the world why the Baptist could not have baptized them. A resurrected being is not going to melt if he gets wet. The point is, they could do it for themselves, and so John had them do it. Then he had them confer on each other the priesthood he had just given them, all over again. Why did he do that? He did it to establish the order of the kingdom and to affirm again that this was now something they could do. It would not be necessary for John to return to perform the ordinance every time someone needed to receive the priesthood (Joseph Smith–History 1:68–74).

We have another wonderful illustration of this principle in the Book of Mormon. When the Jaredites needed to cross the ocean, the Lord told them to build some barges. What he did not tell them was *how* to build the barges. They had already done that kind of thing and did not need instruction on the matter. Nevertheless, they ran into some problems they had never faced before. First, there was the matter of getting air into the barges, so when the brother of Jared took this matter to the Lord, He told him how to solve the problem. Next came the problem of providing light for the barges. Again, the brother of Jared took the problem to the Lord, but this time the Lord did not solve it for him. The brother of Jared had not exhausted his own capacity on this matter, so the Lord said, "What will ye that I should do that ye may have light in your vessels?" (Ether 2:23). They talked about it a little, and the Lord said, "What will ye that I should prepare for you that ye may have light when ye are swallowed up in the depths of the sea?" (Ether 2:25).

This was simply to say, "Why are you troubling me with this matter? You have agency. You can do more than you have done. Think about it and come back with a recommendation for solving this problem."

The brother of Jared did just that. After thinking about it, he took sixteen small, clear stones back to the Lord and asked him to touch them with his finger to put light into them. The Lord did so (Ether 2:19–3:6).

This experience of the brother of Jared takes us back to the Oliver Cowdery story and the principle it illustrates. The formula given there (D&C 9) is that we study the matter out in our minds, meaning we do all that we can to find the proper solution. This may involve all manner of searching and researching, Then, having done our homework, we come to a conclusion or recommendation. When we take our conclusion or recommendation back to the Lord, he will either confirm it or give us a "stupor of thought," intended to bring confusion or forgetfulness so that we will know we must continue our search for an answer.

The meaning of all of this is that when we have problems, we look for solutions, not handouts. Certainly, we search the scriptures, read good books, talk with our parents, and counsel with our priesthood leaders. We realize, however, that it is not the order of the Church for us to simply dump our problems in the laps of our home teachers or the bishop. It is for us to make the journey from Egypt to Sinai, not to get a ride on someone else's back. In that process, the more competent we become in handling the problems along the way, the greater our agency, or our power to act, becomes.

Brigham Young lamented that some fathers sought him out every time one of their children needed a blessing. Should I not do their plowing, planting, and harvesting also, he asked? Was it the Lord's intent in teaching us to pray for our daily bread that we then wait for an angel to deliver it, or did he have in mind that we go and labor for it? "If you learn how to use the agency that God has given you," noted Elder Bruce R. McConkie, "and if you try to make your own decisions, and if you reach conclusions that are sound and right, and you counsel with the Lord and get his ratifying seal of approval upon the conclusions you've reached, then you've received revelation."[1] President Brigham Young explained that when you have sought the direction of heaven on a matter and no clear answer has come but the time for a decision has, you make the best decision you can and the Lord is obligated to honor it as his own.[2]

AGENT OR INSTRUMENT?

Life is balanced by diversity. In some instances we may be a leader; in others, a follower; in some, a teacher, in others, a student. Some occasions call for us to speak up; others demand that we listen quietly. We must both work and rest, give praise and correction, give help and receive help. There are things we should notice, and others that we should ignore.

In short, there are occasions in which we must act, and others in which we are to be acted upon; that is, we are to be both independent and submissive, both agent and instrument.

We find the balance between agency and submission to the will of heaven on the scale that bears the name righteousness. Because it is the light of heaven we seek, we simply pursue the course that places us in the greatest light. To oppose the verities of heaven—whatever the reason—is to wander in darkness. In giving us the gift of agency, God gave us the capacity to find and follow the light.

As an agent we must know when to change and when to hold constant. In many instances it may be wiser to change our attitude than to seek to change our circumstances. While we should have the faith to change the weather, we should also have the sense to change the way we are dressed to accommodate the weather.

As an agent unto ourselves, we have the power of self-action. That is, we determine how we are going to act or what we are going to do. It is, for instance, our prerogative to choose our friends. No one can impose this choice on us. It is also our right to choose whether we will be happy or unhappy, what will offend us and what will make us defensive or angry. Others can push our buttons, but we wire them. In truth, we alone are responsible for our choice of emotions. I read of a man who had an experience of which it was said, "It drove him to drink." I thought it interesting that in the same circumstances others have chosen to turn to God and in the process developed great faith.

The principle is an important one. If you dress immodestly because it is fashionable to do so, you are an instrument, not an agent. You have surrendered your agency to the mythical god of fashion or social pressure. In that situation you may be an agent by actively getting others also to dress immodestly, or you may be simply an instrument—someone to be acted upon—but what you are not is an agent unto yourself.

A few years ago one of my daughters, who was then in junior high school, suggested to her friends that she might come to school dressed contrary to student fashions. They told her she would not dare. She said she would. They said she would not. She got the bet up to ten dollars and accepted it.

Having a pure conscience, she came to me and asked if she tithed the money and then used the rest of it for a birthday present for one of her sisters, would it be all right to take it? I told her it would be the easiest ten dollars she ever earned.

So she went to school dressed contrary to popular fashion—which was probably a somewhat fashionable thing in itself—and got the money. In doing so she learned something about becoming an agent unto herself. Among other things she learned that it can be profitable.

Sustaining Others in the Use
of Their Agency

The power of agency is often best used by those who know when not to use it and instead sustain others in using their agency. If the kingdom of heaven is enhanced by all of its inhabitants having agency, surely we could reason that we can only truly strengthen our own dominion by allowing all within it full use of their agency.

A recent book on Joseph Smith by a man of secular acclaim described the Prophet as a benevolent dictator who sought to control every facet of his follower's lives. In so saying the writer evidenced that he missed the true genius of the man of whom he wrote. "God hath not revealed anything to Joseph," the Prophet said, "but what He will make known unto the Twelve, and even the least Saint may know all things as fast as he is able to bear them."[3]

It was through Joseph Smith that the doctrine of common consent was established, the authority restored by which the gift of the Holy Ghost could be given to all members of the Church (which includes the right of personal revelation), the priesthood given to all worthy males, and the doctrine of joint-heirship again established on the earth—the doctrine by which the key is turned so that all may become equal with God "in power, and in might, and in dominion" (D&C

76:95). Earth has never known an egalitarian movement to match the restored gospel. Never have a people stood so equal with their leaders. "I teach the people correct principles," Joseph Smith said, "and they govern themselves."[4]

The irony in the complaint that the Church seeks to limit the agency of its members is that this complaint always comes from those who seek to rob the Saints of their agency. Those doing the complaining invariably want support in some debilitating activity that has resulted in the loss of a good share of their own agency. Now they want others to join them so they will not appear as stupid as they really are.

As the night must balance the day and the day the night, so agency and inspiration must balance each other. Their companionship is as fixed and as eternal as truth and righteousness or as faith and repentance.

CHAPTER SIX

ENEMIES OF AGENCY

Behold, here am I, send me, I will be thy son, and I will redeem all mankind, that one soul shall not be lost, and surely I will do it; wherefore give me thine honor.
LUCIFER (MOSES 4:1)

Even while we were in our premortal estate, Satan "sought to destroy the agency of man" (Moses 4:3). His efforts to do so were cloaked in the guise of a universal salvation in which he as the Son of God would "redeem all mankind," that not so much as "one soul" would be lost (Moses 4:1). In addition, he sought the honor, or power, of the Father so that he might rule and reign over all things. When the Father chose the Firstborn to be his Only Begotten in the flesh, Satan rebelled and turned a third of the host of heaven against God "because of their agency" (D&C 29:36). All that so rebelled were thrust out of the heavens to become "the devil and his angels" (D&C 29:37).

No more dramatic illustration could be given of the importance of agency than that found in these events. We need only imagine gathering everyone we love into a grand assembly and then casting out one-third of that number under conditions that would never admit a reconciliation. All who sided with Satan were hopelessly lost. Yet it could be no other way. God could no more deny the right of choice to his children than he could repudiate all that was good and right, favoring instead wickedness and sin.

In this matter God had no choice. There was no decision to be made, no compromise or middle ground to be found. Compliance with the plan whereby salvation comes must be a freewill offering or it is no offering at all. Freedom and righteousness are the parents of all other gospel principles. No principles can claim life without them. Thus in the family of gospel principles, agency is the firstborn and the life and light of all the other principles.

ALL THAT IS UNCLEAN

It naturally follows that the legions of darkness have declared an everlasting war against the doctrine of agency and seek to destroy or distort it in any way they can. To whatever degree we fall into the bondage of sin, the victory is theirs. Consider the Word of Wisdom. To be high on drugs is to be low on agency. It is to have surrendered the right to control and govern one's own actions. Though addictions come in all shapes and sizes, they are always recognizable by the way they determine or control our actions.

All that is unclean is offensive to the Spirit. The Spirit is light, and that which stands opposite it is dark. You cannot move into the dark without moving out of the light. No other choice is possible. We commonly hear people argue that they can do things the Brethren have said are offensive to the Spirit without losing the Spirit. In so saying they deceive only themselves. Elder George A. Smith illustrated this point with a story about a man named John Smith. It seems that this fellow got up in a meeting and said "he had proved the revelations of Joseph Smith to be untrue. 'How did you prove them so?' 'Why,' said he, 'one of Joseph Smith's revelations says, that if a man shall commit adultery, he shall lose the Spirit of the Lord, and deny the faith, and shall be cast out. Now,' says he, 'I have been guilty of that crime, and I have not apostatized, and consequently that revelation is not true, and that proves Joseph Smith is not a true Prophet.'"[1]

Similarly, it is true that no strength may be found in dependency relationships. The more dependent we are—that is, the less power we have to act for ourselves—the smaller the claim we have to agency. Knowledge of truth and training and the confidence that comes from them expand our agency. Conversely, ignorance is a form of bondage. "Know the truth," the Savior said, "and the truth shall make you free" (John 8:32). He was not referring to the knowledge of mathematics, chemistry, or ancient languages, though the knowledge of each of these brings with it a degree of freedom. The truth to which Christ had reference was that of his own messianic office. The essential truth of which he was speaking is the knowledge that he is indeed the Son of God, the promised Messiah, and that salvation is in him and in none other.

INTEGRITY OF OUR INTENT

Laws are and always have been necessary to the preservation of society. Surely we are within the mark to suppose that as long as there have been laws, there have been those who have seen those laws as a form of constraint and have chosen to violate them. The issue is whether such a course brings greater freedom or not. Obviously, if everyone chooses to break the law, chaos reigns where it was hoped the law would bring order and safety. But what of the individuals who choose to flout the law? Are they increasing their power of action by so doing? It certainly appears that they do, or there would be no temptation to disobey the law in the first place.

The great variety of laws and circumstances make a simple answer to such a question difficult if not impossible. Such an answer would have to suppose that all laws are wise and proper, which is not the case. This much, however, can be said with perfect confidence: The spirit that attends the indiscriminate or habitual breaking of laws will ultimately bring its own retribution. We can make no decisions relative to the keeping or breaking of laws that will not either strengthen or weaken our character. The cumulative effect of such decisions can be depended on at some future time to either bless us or curse us.

The integrity of our intent is of great importance in God's system of justice. Indeed, the scriptures tell us that we will not be judged by our works alone but rather by our works and our desires. This means that even though our works have the appearance of gold, their true meaning will not be ascertained until the true desires of our heart have been taken into account. Thus, the man who commits adultery in his heart and would have done so in the flesh had he found a willing partner will be rewarded as if he had acted on his adulterous thoughts. Conversely, the woman who has never married or raised a family because of circumstances beyond her control but would have done so had an appropriate opportunity come to her will yet be granted that privilege. She will be rewarded for her efforts in this life as if she had been married and borne children.

The principle is simply this: In all the eternities there never will be a worthy man or woman whose righteous desires were denied them in this life because of circumstances beyond their control who will not have those privileges accorded to them in the worlds to come. On the other hand, no one is going to get away with anything, regardless of how cleverly they hid the evil desires of their souls. None will have cause to question the justice of God.

RIGHT REASONS

When the dust settles on the great battles of life, what matters is not whether we won or lost but where and how we fought. There will always be other battles to follow, and the strength of character we take with us into these battles will already have been determined. Those who surrender their honor and integrity can hardly expect to depend upon the same.

Elder Marion G. Romney expressed this principle thus: "When the issues are determined, whether we stand with the winners or the losers, of this we may be sure: To make the proper choice on any issue is of far more importance to us personally than is the immediate outcome of the issue upon which we make a decision. The choices we make will affect the scope of our agency in the future. As of now, we have the right of decision. What we will have tomorrow depends upon how we decide today."[2]

There is something very important about doing the right thing for the right reason. In taking true-and-false tests, students quickly learn that if part of the statement is false, the entire statement is false. So it is in life. It will not do to hide a rotten apple at the bottom of the barrel, supposing that surrounding it with good apples will negate its rottenness. Quite the contrary. If we are doing things for the wrong reason, everything we do becomes wrong. Our wrong reason could be likened to a drop of ink in a glass of clear water. It quickly diffuses, polluting all of the water. We cannot come back later and strain it out.

TUMULT OF OPINIONS

Any gospel principle presented in such a manner that it promises salvation without obligation is at odds with both the order of heaven and the principle of agency. Such an argument violates the order of heaven because we have been promised that we will be judged by our works. It violates the principle of agency because our works are the only true measure of our profession to follow and believe. Everything we choose to do or not to do is based on our belief system.

It stands to reason that the idea of salvation by grace without works will be most appealing to those who have little by way of works to represent them. This may explain why a third part of the premortal host chose to follow Lucifer and his guarantee of salvation with no requirement of righteousness or obedience. The works of the premortal life follow us into this life and, like a mirror, reflect our likeness.

Among mortals Satan has his own prophets and apostles who are teaching and advocating his doctrine. "All mankind should be saved at the last day," taught Nehor, "and that they need not fear nor tremble, but that they might lift up their heads and rejoice; for the Lord had created all men, and had also redeemed all men; and, in the end, all men should have eternal life" (Alma 1:4). If the word were to go forth to the laborers in the vineyard that remuneration was to be granted to those who praised their Master, not those who honored him by laboring to harvest his fruit, who then would labor?

Amidst the "war of words" and the "tumult of opinions" (Joseph Smith–History 1:10) in the world of religion, some argue passionately that there are two churches: the church of law and the church of love. The church of law is depicted as hard, unfeeling, bigoted, arrogant, intolerant, rigid, and mean-spirited because it declares that God is law and that there are requirements that must be complied with to enter into the kingdom of heaven.

By contrast, they argue, in the church of love it does not matter what you believe or with what denomination you affiliate. The only thing of concern is whether you are loving or not. For them the great questions are these: Are you open and respectful of others? Are you kind and tolerant of all behavior and belief systems (except, of course, those that advocate the necessity of law)? The church of love does not countenance the idea of priesthood or of anyone having authority over anyone else. It holds that Christian doctrine was developed after the time of Christ and was not a part of pure Christianity as he established it. By nature it believes doctrine to be both divisive and intolerant and thus at odds with the message of Christ. True Christianity, meaning the Christianity instituted by Christ—according to the disciples of the church of love— did not extend beyond acceptance, tolerance, and love. Ordinances, doctrines, and requirements of any sort, they hold, are corruptions of a later date. Scriptures stating otherwise (of which there are many) are held to be interpolations by evil and designing men. Christianity is reduced to a single doctrine, "the unconditional love of God," which spokespersons for the church of love tell us was manifest to us through Christ. Thus, that which they call God's unconditional love provides, in their minds, justification for all that is impure, unholy, or ungodly. To be critical of such behavior makes one both judgmental and intolerant, which are the only real sins according to the advocates of this sect.

Yet we know that the God of Israel announced himself to be holy and declared for that reason his people must also be holy. The followers of Christ were known as disciples, which means disciplined followers. No doctrine was better understood among them than that no unclean thing can enter the presence of God. Everything in the law of Moses was designed to teach this, as are all the ordinances of the gospel known to the Saints of the New Testament. The fundamental doctrine of both the Old and New Testament is that we came into the world to fight against our fallen nature, not to fall in love with it.

Even within The Church of Jesus Christ of Latter-day Saints we find those who espouse (usually unknowingly) the principles of the church of love. The dangers of their theology, even if innocent and well intended, are nevertheless quite real. God's love is perfect, but it is not unconditional. For instance, a woman cannot marry a man and then share herself equally with all men. True, she is to have a love for all mankind, but it is not the same kind of love that she shares with her companion and spouse. To confuse the two would be disastrous to her soul, not to mention her marriage. There is a kind of love that she shares with her husband that she cannot share with someone of her own gender. With her husband she can share a perfect love but only in a covenant relationship—and all covenants require conditions. So it is with our relationship with God. It is a covenant relationship, we are a covenant people, and covenants contain conditions, outside of which the love we share with God and Christ cannot be perfect.

It must be said quite clearly that it is a false dichotomy to suppose there is a church of law and a church of love. Law cannot stand independent of love, for it was born of it. All societies require laws, limits, and bounds to the behavior of its citizens. These laws may include everything from how fast we drive in residential areas to what kind of pesticides we use. The commonality in all these laws is a respect for the sanctity of life and the protection of the innocent. Laws are thus an expression of love. The kingdom of God is no less a place of order, decency, and love. By definition God can be neither lawless nor passionless but rather must possess both in their perfection. To argue that law and love are incompatible is to argue that justice and mercy are incompatible; in reality, without the one we cannot have the other.

A Perfect Expression of the Principles of Agency

Revelation affords no more perfect expression of the principle of agency than that found in the instructions given on how the authority of the priesthood is to be used. "The rights of the priesthood," we are told, "are inseparably connected with the powers of heaven, and . . . cannot be controlled nor handled only upon the principles of righteousness. That they may be conferred upon us, it is true; but when we undertake to cover our sins, or to gratify our pride, our vain ambition, or to exercise control or dominion or compulsion upon the souls of the children of men, in any degree of unrighteousness, behold, the heavens withdraw themselves; the Spirit of the Lord is grieved; and when it is withdrawn, Amen to the priesthood or the authority of that man" (D&C 121:36–37).

This revelation—which, ironically, was penned by the Prophet while he was a prisoner in the Liberty Jail—states that "no power or influence can or ought to be maintained by virtue of the priesthood, only by persuasion, by long-suffering, by gentleness and meekness, and by love unfeigned; by kindness, and pure knowledge, which shall greatly enlarge the soul without hypocrisy, and without guile—reproving betimes with sharpness, when moved upon by the Holy Ghost; and then showing forth afterwards an increase of love toward him whom thou hast reproved, lest he esteem thee to be his enemy" (D&C 121:41–43).

CHAPTER SEVEN

AGENCY AND THE LAW OF CONSEQUENCES

There is a law, irrevocably decreed in heaven before the foundations
of this world, upon which all blessings are predicated—
and when we obtain any blessing from God, it is by
obedience to that law upon which it is predicated.
DOCTRINE & COVENANTS 130:20–21

Perhaps all of us at one time or another have besought the heavens, pleading to be spared the consequences of our actions. How often have students who lacked the discipline to study and prepare properly for a test prayed for help in taking the examination? Or athletes who failed to practice or train properly importuned the heavens to make up the difference? What of Sunday School teachers or sacrament meeting speakers who, having failed to prepare, announces they are going to rely on the Spirit? What of individuals, now deathly ill, seeking priesthood blessings after years of abusing their bodies? Are they not somewhat akin to a farmer who fails to plant the seed and yet seeks through his faith to have a rich harvest?

Surely a God of miracles, the God who created this earth and all that is on it, the Almighty God by whose hand all men will be resurrected, would not find any such situations too difficult to change. But then again, what right do we have to ask God to make up for our willful negligence and do for us what we could have done for ourselves? Would his doing so in truth be godly, or would its effect be to weaken men and rob them of the endowment of agency he has already given them?

In response to such questions, Elder Robert S. Wood of the Second Quorum of Seventy notes: "Ancient Greek dramatists had a device they used when the characters in their dramas were trapped in a complex web of dilemmas, largely of their own making—the *deus ex machina*. This was a machine in which actors portraying the gods would suddenly be lowered on the scene to save the mortal characters from the consequences of their own actions. . . . The psychologist Erich Fromm called the wish to escape the consequences of one's actions a desire to escape from freedom."[1] The matter reduces itself to the question, Can there be freedom without responsibility?

Lehi gives powerful expression to the principles here involved, "Wherefore, men are free according to the flesh; and all things are given them which are expedient unto man. And they are free to choose liberty and eternal life, through the great Mediator of all men, or to choose captivity and death, according to the captivity and power of the devil; for he seeketh that all men might be miserable like unto himself" (2 Nephi 2:27).

PICKING UP THE STICK

There is no stick that does not have two ends. If you pick up one end, you have also picked up the other. So it is that there are no choices without consequences. Every choice to do something is at the same time a choice not to do something else. We cannot march in opposing armies. We cannot be both a Philistine and an Israelite. If we choose to march with the army of Israel, we have chosen not to advocate Philistine causes. If our covenant is to be a Latter-day Saint, then we have no right to teach or write or advocate that which is in opposition to the Church. As an employee of Brigham Young University, I do not have the right to ridicule and fight my employer. Some argue that this condition compromises academic freedom. It does not. Only at such a privately owned university do I have the right to teach the classes in religion that I teach. I cannot teach them at a state-owned school. If I choose to teach at a state-owned school, I surrender this right and I have no business complaining about it.

Once again we are reduced to the verity that all choices are bound to consequences. Good choices bring opportunities, but such opportunities always demand something in return. The greater the opportunity, the greater the responsibility. At issue in the minds of some is whether a loving and merciful God could refuse their petition to spare them the rightful consequences of their actions. Another way of asking this question is, Are there occasions in which we can induce God to break his own laws or go back on his own word? If, for instance, you rejected the ordinance of baptism, could you in faith pray and ask God to suspend the necessity of that ordinance because your being baptized would be offensive to your mother, who would be embarrassed by your becoming a Mormon? Given that we would have little expectation of a positive response to such a plea, we might instead want to plead for a waiver of the necessity of our repenting of our sins before being baptized. Again, because the probability of receiving a positive response to such a petition is not great, we might opt for a waiver of specific and particular sins that in our judgment could not possibly do any harm to anyone else. Though this may seem silly, people are in effect constantly doing it.

When people seek the help of heaven in excusing them from the consequences of their actions, what they are really doing is asking God to cease being God and do something less than godly in their case, with the idea in mind that if he will do so, they will truly know that he is God. The picture simply does not hang straight.

Would we not be better served to seek to change our own nature rather than God's? As long as we retain the power of choice, we can improve our circumstances. If we have not procrastinated our repentance until it is "everlastingly too late" (Helaman 13:38), we can change our course, pay the penalty for our transgressions, and through the grace of Christ claim the reward of our works, and, to whatever extent they allow, become "heirs of salvation" (D&C 138:59).

THE LAW OF CONSEQUENCES

The law of consequences is taught to us in scripture with unequaled plainness. "There is a law, irrevocably decreed in heaven before the foundations of this world, upon which all blessings are predicated—and when we obtain any blessing from God, it is by obedience to that law upon which it is predicated" (D&C 130:20–21). Again we are told, "For all who will have a blessing at my hands shall abide the law which was appointed for that blessing, and the conditions thereof, as were instituted from before the foundation of the world" (D&C 132:5). No one can escape these principles. They operate the same in this, our second estate, as they did in our premortal life, and they will continue to operate in the same manner throughout the endless eternities. Surely one of the great evidences of apostate Christianity is the idea that by professing Christ, we can escape the consequences of our actions. On the contrary, to accept Christ is to accept responsibility for our actions. It is in Christ that we seek the strength to correct all that needs correcting, for as Alma taught, "Repentance could not come unto men except there were a punishment, which also was eternal as the life of the soul should be, affixed opposite to the plan of happiness, which was as eternal also as the life of the soul. Now, how could a man repent except he should sin? How could he sin if there was no law? How could there be a law save there was a punishment?" (Alma 42:16–17).

Jesus, in his parable of the prodigal son, gives a classic illustration of the immutable effects of law. "You will remember that in it," noted Elder Marion G. Romney, "a young man, exercising his inherent right of choice, makes a decision to take his portion of his father's estate and go and see the world. This he does, whereupon nature follows its uniform course. When the prodigal's substance is squandered, he makes another choice, which takes him back home where he meets 'the ring, and the robe, and the fatted calf.' His felicitous father gives him a welcome. But the consequence of his earlier decision 'is following him up, for the farm is gone. The "father" himself cannot undo the effect of the foregone choice.' (Collins, *Such Is Life,* pp. 85–88.)"[2]

Who and what we were yesterday determines who and what we are today. A Sumo wrestler has no worry that he is going to go to bed and wake up a ballet dancer, and a ballet dancer has no worry that she is going to go to bed and wake up a Sumo wrestler. The question is often asked, To what extent do the choices we made in the premortal life affect who and what we are in this life? The answer is easily found by asking another question: To what extent do the choices we make in this life affect who and what we will be in the life to come?

We reap as we have sown.

THE EVIL OF DEPENDENCY RELATIONSHIPS

Where character and gospel principles are concerned, there are no shortcuts. This truth is simply a manifestation of the verity that we reap as we have sown and the consequences of our actions are immutable. Let us suppose for a moment that a newly called bishop, a man of considerable means who possesses great sympathy and love, surveys his ward and discovers that many families were deeply in debt. Suppose that quietly and privately he goes to each of these families, determines the extent of their indebtedness, and gives them the money to pay it all off. Let us then suppose that he goes back to each of these families a year later to see how they are doing. What would he find? Would he discover that he was now presiding over a ward in which there was no indebtedness? Or would he find the same people nurturing the same problems? Would he find that among their number were some who had their hands extended, expecting more help? And would some of these take offense if the help was not forthcoming?

If this good bishop is going to make a difference, he, like von Steuben at Valley Forge, must teach discipline. Again this takes us back to the need for balance or harmony in gospel principles. The bishop's generosity, independent of the needed discipline and restraint on the part of those he seeks to help, would weaken rather than strengthen them. Simply stated, money is not the solution to money problems.

Having discovered that his efforts to guarantee the temporal salvation of his ward members is unsuccessful, let us suppose that the good bishop decides to redirect his efforts to matters of the Spirit. Having so decided, he makes another round of visits. This time as he sits in council with each of his ward members, he seeks to discover the matters upon which they need divine direction. Let us further suppose that he then seeks and obtains that direction for them. Now, having placed every household in the ward in order, he hopes to go home and relax, knowing that all is well in Zion. To his disappointment, however, he soon learns that a new set of dilemmas has replaced the old ones and that his ward members are as help-less to solve their problems as they were before his round of visits. So it is that he learns he cannot work out the spiritual salvation of his ward members any more than he can work out their temporal salvation. His role, he will learn, is to teach cor-rect principles, but of necessity he must let the members of the ward govern themselves.

It has wisely been observed that teachers have succeeded when their students no longer need them. Bishops are teach-ers, and they have succeeded when the members of their ward no longer have to lean on them for help, be it temporal or spiri-tual. A good bishop does not train the members of his ward to come to him when they need the direction of the Spirit. Rather, he teaches them how to get that inspiration for themselves. The companionship of the Holy Ghost is promised to every mem-ber of the Church—not just to bishops. If we become spiritu-ally dependent on the bishop, we surrender our God-given gift of agency. It might seem a comfortable thing, for instance, for a young woman to take to her bishop the decision about whom she should marry, because then if the marriage does not work out, it can be his fault, not hers. That, however, is not the order of the kingdom. In marriage, as in all other things, we are responsible for our own decisions, and we will reap the conse-quences of those decisions, be they happy or sad.

Recently, my wife and I spoke by assignment to the young

men and young women in our stake. It was a stake standards night. As we entered the chapel, we were handed a little stack of papers on which were written questions the young people wanted answers to. There was an interesting variety of questions, such as, What constitutes a date? Why no dating before the age of sixteen? What was wrong with sleeveless outfits? And so forth. I spoke to them briefly about the principle of agency and then invited my wife to field some of their questions. The answers she gave clearly evidenced that she was a loving and wise mother. After she had answered a few questions, she said in effect, "We may not be doing the right thing here. You cannot wait every year for a stake standards night to get answers to your questions. What we need to do is teach you the standards, and then you can answer these questions for yourselves."

Her observation was obviously inspired by the Spirit. Although it might have helped to have us clarify the reasons for the standards and reassure the young people that those standards constitute the only safe path, teaching them how to answer their own questions was more important than any answer that we could give them.

Escaping Freedom

The attempt to escape the consequences of our actions is at best an attempt to escape freedom. Dostoyevsky, in his work

The Brothers Karamazov, has a marvelously insightful chapter entitled "The Grand Inquisitor." His story takes place in the sixteenth century in a world ruled by the Roman Catholic Church. In this story Christ quietly returns to earth and raises a little girl from the dead, for which action he is arrested by the cardinal who is the Grand Inquisitor. What follows is a one-sided conversation in which the cardinal explains why he must once again condemn Christ to death. He begins by berating Christ for having granted freedom to His followers. Turn stones to bread, the Inquisitor says, and mankind will run after you like "'a flock of sheep, grateful and obedient, forever trembling, lest Thou withdraw Thy hand and deny them Thy bread.' But Thou wouldst not deprive man of freedom," he says to Christ, "and didst reject the offer, thinking, what is that freedom worth, if obedience is bought with bread? Thou didst reply that man lives not by bread alone. But dost Thou know that for the sake of that earthly bread the spirit of the earth will rise up against Thee and will strive with Thee and overcome Thee? And all will follow him, crying: 'Who can compare with this beast? He has given us fire from heaven!' Dost Thou know that the ages will pass, and humanity will proclaim by the lips of their sages that there is no crime, and therefore no sin; there is only hunger? 'Feed men, and then ask of them virtue!' that's what they'll write on the banner, which they will raise against Thee, and with which they will destroy Thy temple. Where Thy temple stood will rise a new building: the terrible tower of Babel will be built again. . . . They are sinful and rebellious, but in the end they too will become obedient. They will marvel at us and look on us as gods, because we are ready to endure the Freedom which they have found so dreadful and to rule over them—so awful will it seem to them to be free. But we shall tell them that we are Thy servants and rule them in Thy name. We shall deceive them again, for we will not let Thee come to us again. That deception will be our suffering, for we shall be forced to lie. . . . Didst Thou forget that man prefers peace, and even death, to freedom of choice in the knowledge of good and evil? Nothing is more seductive for man than his freedom of conscience, but nothing is a greater cause of suffering."[3]

So it is that the cardinal argues that his people had surrendered their freedom for the promise of bread and their agency for the promise of salvation. Such was the tragic mistake of those who chose to follow Lucifer in the Grand Council of Heaven. There is great danger in the pursuit of security, be it temporal or spiritual. We must weigh carefully all promises that offer security at the cost of some measure of our freedom. Any commitment we might be tempted to make that does not increase our power to act in a positive way is not of God.

To surrender our right to act for ourselves, even in small

ways, is to invite that spirit which seeks our enslavement. Consider how most Latter-day Saints go about preparing a talk to be given in church. Having been assigned a subject, they seek out what others have said about it. They then take their collection of quotations and organize them to fit the time constraints they have been given. They feel safe and secure in giving their talk because they are only repeating what others who held positions of authority have said. While the form of such talks is generally excellent, they may lack spiritual power and conviction. That power and conviction comes only when those giving the talk first search their own heart and mind. Only after they have done so can they can they take the scriptures and personalize them or make them their own.

In some instances quotations from others are helpful, but they are not a substitute for the speakers' own responsibility to think, feel, and pray. Such quotations are simply a second witness to that which they have come to know. Generally, however, we quote others for security. We are shifting the responsibility for the doctrine from ourselves to them. In doing so we may also be shifting the responsibility to them to think, feel, pray, and understand. Perhaps that is what the Savior had in mind when he warned against vain repetition. The net effect of such shifting is that we come to feel that knowledge and understanding belong to an office, one that we do not hold. It is therefore out of our grasp, and we are not responsible for it.

In the sectarian world the result is a corruption of the Lord's system of worship. There the priest or minister does the praying for the congregation and that too, frequently, from written or prescribed prayers. This is bread without leaven. The responsibility to do the preaching or the teaching also rests with the hireling. Again the congregation is excused— they have paid to have someone else do this for them. In being so excused, they surrender a significant portion of their God-given agency. If such a system really worked, we could also hire people to work out for us so that we can remain in good physical condition.

In the Church we can find ourselves parroting instead of thinking, under the guise of following the Brethren. If, however, we were really following the Brethren, we would do what they do—which is to share what they have learned firsthand, instead of relying on others. To see what is involved, consider what would happen if a young man followed the same procedure in a courtship. First, he would conduct a search to see what others have said and written to their beloved. He would then select from this material, organize it nicely, and present it to the young woman he intended to court. The problem is that if the young woman involved has any sense, she will fall in love with the original writer and tell the courier to get lost.

Faith Requires Truth

It is a law of heaven that all gospel principles act in harmony with each other. Faith and truth, for instance, cannot function independent of each other. Thus, faith cannot be exercised in false principles. We cannot suppose that a person's sincerity or the great love that God has for him can supplant these laws. To imbibe poison while sincerely believing it to be harmless will not negate its effects. To sincerely worship a false god will not open the windows of heaven to the worshipper.

Scripture refers to ordinances performed without priesthood authority as "dead works" (D&C 22:2). For all ordinances to be of "efficacy, virtue, or force in and after the resurrection from the dead," they must be ratified or approved by the Holy Spirit of promise (D&C 132:7). That ratifying seal will not be placed upon the ordinances unless we have lived up to them with exactness and honor. There will be no cheats or liars in heaven, no hypocrites or feigned piety. Nor will there be any who have escaped the consequences of their actions.

CHAPTER EIGHT

AGENCY AND ITS SEASONS

And again, verily I say unto you, he hath given a law unto all things,
by which they move in their times and their seasons.
DOCTRINE & COVENANTS 88:42

As a priesthood leader, I have spent hours and hours in various training sessions. A theme common to such meetings is that we are to so conduct ourselves that we might be instruments in the hands of the Lord. In most Church callings the nature of our duties is clearly spelled out. Though there is latitude for individual differences and variations in circumstances, the nature of our callings is essentially the same, regardless of the ward or stake in which we reside. Thus, the nature of the office or calling dictates our actions. As we conform to the duties of our calling and get in tune with the Spirit of the

Lord, we become instruments in his hands. That is, the Lord uses us as he chooses.

Scripture also speaks of our being agents, or agents unto ourselves. An agent differs from an instrument in that the responsibility to determine an agent's actions has not been predetermined. There is no handbook that tells us how to be an agent or gives a list of duties that we as agents are to perform. The agent makes such determinations. An agent chooses how he or she will serve rather than having that determination made by an office or position they hold.

We cannot be an instrument and an agent at the same time. Each must have its time and season, and with the changing of the seasons comes the opportunity for us to find newness of life and energy. In such a circumstance the Lord gets a good measure of our spiritual maturity. It is a sad commentary when someone slips into inactivity after being released from a position of responsibility. To serve well as an instrument but not as an agent is something akin to the person who works well when closely supervised but who cannot be trusted to work well when left on his own.

Agency and Accountability

Agency is a gift of God that we bring with us into this world and, like the talents that we also brought, lies dormant within our soul, waiting to be developed. Its growth and expression parallel that of accountability. Some have falsely supposed that children are not accountable until they are eight years of age. That is not what the revelations teach. Rather, they teach that a child is sufficiently accountable before the Lord at the age of eight to know right from wrong, to know Jesus is the Christ, and to assume the covenant of baptism. No one would suppose, however, that at the age of eight they are sufficiently accountable to marry or to move away and live on their own. At the age of six (in our society), they are deemed sufficiently accountable to attend school, where they are expected to act in a responsible manner. Well before their children reach that age, parents begin teaching them various degrees of accountability, even before the children begin to walk.

The language of the scriptures is clear. In June 1829 the Lord told Joseph Smith that "all men must repent and be baptized, and not only men, but women, and children who have arrived at the years of accountability" (D&C 18:42). Note that the text reads "years," not year, of accountability.

In September 1830 the Lord explained: "Little children are redeemed from the foundation of the world through mine Only Begotten; wherefore, they cannot sin, for power is not given unto Satan to tempt little children"—now note the language—"until they begin to become accountable before me"

(D&C 29:46–47). That is to say, as children begin to be accountable, they also begin to become subject to temptation. Temptation shadows accountability.

In November 1831 this instruction was given: "And again, inasmuch as parents have children in Zion, or in any of her stakes which are organized, that teach them not to understand the doctrine of repentance, faith in Christ the Son of the living God, and of baptism and the gift of the Holy Ghost by the laying on of the hands, when eight years old, the sin be upon the heads of the parents. For this shall be a law unto the inhabitants of Zion, or in any of her stakes which are organized. And their children shall be baptized for the remission of their sins when eight years old, and receive the laying on of the hands" (D&C 68:25–27).

Now, it is reasonable to suppose that if children are to be baptized at the age of eight for the "remission of their sins," they must have some sins that need remitting. That is not to suppose that such sins would be of a serious or grievous nature, but it is reasonable to suppose that in the process of growing up into the accountability that precedes baptism, they erred in one way or another.

I rehearse this matter of the accountability of little children as an illustration of the fact that the accountability that shadows agency is a process, not an event. The agency of a child is not the same as that of an adult, any more than the degree of accountability is the same. We grow up into both. Agency and accountability have their own times and seasons.

THE GIFT WILLINGLY GIVEN

When God sought from among the host of heaven one whose labor would be to redeem the rest of his children, he made the selection of the Savior himself an expression of the right of choice by asking, "Whom shall I send?" When the Firstborn said, "Here am I, send me" (Abraham 3:27), his was a freewill offering and thus accorded with the order of heaven, for all that is acceptable in heaven must be freely given. Thus, in his mortal ministry Christ made frequent reference to the fact that he sought not his own will but "the will of the Father," who, he said, "hath sent me" (John 5:30). "I came down from heaven, not to do mine own will, but the will of him that sent me" (John 6:38). Thus, as Abinadi expressed it, the will of the Son was "swallowed up in the will of the Father" (Mosiah 15:7). So it was that in that matchless prayer offered in Gethsemane, Christ prayed, "Abba, Father, all things are possible unto thee; take away this cup from me: nevertheless not what I will, but what thou wilt" (Mark 14:36). And finally, on the cross just before he yielded up the ghost, he said, "Father, it is finished, thy will is done" (JST Matthew 27:50).

In all of this Christ establishes the system and plan of salvation, which consists of our becoming one with him and with the Father. We have been saved to the extent that we have learned to think as they think, believe as they believe, and act as they act. It is a matter of our accepting the sacred gift of agency and willingly returning it to the Lord, for only in the paradox of that process does the gift become truly ours.

Elder Boyd K. Packer described the process thus: "I knew what agency was and knew how important it was to be individual and to be independent, to be free. I somehow knew there was one thing the Lord would never take from me, and that was my free agency. I would not surrender my agency to any being but to Him! I determined that I would *give* Him the one thing that He would never take—my agency. I decided, by myself, that from that time on I would do things His way.

"That was a great trial for me, for I thought I was giving away the most precious thing I possessed. I was not wise enough in my youth to know that because I exercised my agency and decided myself, I was not *losing* it. It was *strengthened!*

"I learned from that experience the meaning of the scripture: 'If ye continue in my word, then are ye my disciples indeed;

"'And ye shall know the truth, and the truth shall make you free. (John 8:31–32.)'"[1]

112

Thus, in the seasons of agency, we grow up into this matchless gift of God, and, having obtained it, we return it to the Lord. This matter is a process. It is something we repeat each time we enter into covenant with him and then seek to live according to the agreed-upon pattern. And, according to that pattern, he returns the gift to us.

CHAPTER NINE

THE GIFT OF GOD

*What doth it profit a man if a gift is bestowed upon him, and he receive
not the gift? Behold, he rejoices not in that which is given unto
him, neither rejoices in him who is the giver of the gift.*
DOCTRINE & COVENANTS 88:33

What, then, is the doctrine of agency? And what difference
does it make?

Agency is the gift of God given with life itself; it is the
assurance that the power is in us to control our own destiny. It
includes the right in every circumstance of life to choose how
we will respond, where we will stand, and what we will do. It
is the power to act. It makes life our choice. It is the opportunity to be true, to stand and be counted, to contribute to great
causes, to lead and to follow, to cheer and to be cheered, to
create and to rejoice in that which has been created. Whether
we are great or small, as the world measures such things,

agency gives all the sons and daughters of God equal right to call upon the powers of heaven.

Having created the earth and placed Adam and Eve on it, "God blessed them, and God said unto them, Be fruitful, and multiply, and replenish the earth, and subdue it: and have dominion over the fish of the sea, and over the fowl of the air, and over every living thing that moveth upon the earth" (Genesis 1:28). That is, God blessed them with the gift of agency and said, in effect, "Be fruitful, and multiply, build and create, subdue and bring order; all that is right and good and positive is within your capacity to do and I will bless you with the power to do it."

INCREASING OUR POWER TO ACT

To live is to have needs and desires. Our ability to meet those needs, or the power to act, is called agency. The extent of our agency is measured in our ability to respond to those needs and desires. Divine laws direct and control how we increase our power of action, or our agency. Be the matter temporal or spiritual, the principles are the same. These principles include the law of consequences, as we have discussed. The basic idea is that there are no twilight zones in which what we do does not matter. Indeed, everything we do has its effect on who and what we are. As Elder Marion G. Romney noted:

"Every choice one makes either expands or contracts the area in which he [or she] can make and implement future decisions. When one makes a choice, he irrevocably binds himself to accept the consequences of that choice."[1]

A common aphorism, for instance, states that knowledge is power. That is a universal truth. The power of expression demands a command of language, and the greater our command of language, the greater our power of expression. In like manner, we cannot express ourselves effectively in the visual arts without a meaningful understanding of such relationships as color, light, and form. And by the same token, the laws of sound govern expressions in the realm of music. Whatever the field, there are laws that govern it, and the greater our ability to conform to those laws, the greater our ability to perform in that field.

In the realm of spiritual things, knowledge precedes faith. We cannot worship God unless we first know that there is a God to worship. We cannot get answers to prayer until we understand how the Spirit of revelation functions. We must know and live the principle before we can obtain the blessings that flow from it. Thus, the Savior said, "My doctrine is not mine, but his that sent me. If any man will do his will, he shall know of the doctrine, whether it be of God, or whether I speak of myself" (John 7:16–17).

The primary ingredient in our efforts to increase our

agency in the realm of spiritual things is righteousness. It will be recalled that when the angel of the Lord appeared to Cornelius, the angel said that he did so because Cornelius's "alms" were as "a memorial before God" (Acts 10:4). The charge to the holder of the priesthood is that his heart "be full of charity towards all men, and to the household of faith, and let virtue garnish thy thoughts unceasingly; then shall thy confidence wax strong in the presence of God; and the doctrine of the priesthood shall distil upon thy soul as the dews from heaven. The Holy Ghost shall be thy constant companion, and thy scepter an unchanging scepter of righteousness and truth; and thy dominion shall be an everlasting dominion, and without compulsory means it shall flow unto thee forever and ever" (D&C 121:45–46).

One of the great purposes of scripture is to provide us with patterns or examples of what we are to be and to acquaint us with the spiritual powers we can obtain. To Enoch the Lord said, "All thy words will I justify; and the mountains shall flee before you, and the rivers shall turn from their course; and thou shalt abide in me, and I in you; therefore walk with me" (Moses 6:34). In like manner, Nephi, son of Helaman, was told: "Blessed art thou, Nephi, for those things which thou hast done; for I have beheld how thou hast with unwearyingness declared the word, which I have given unto thee, unto this people. And thou hast not feared them, and hast not sought thine own life, but hast sought my will, and to keep my commandments. And now, because thou hast done this with such unwearyingness, behold, I will bless thee forever; and I will make thee mighty in word and in deed, in faith and in works; yea, even that all things shall be done unto thee according to thy word, for thou shalt not ask that which is contrary to my will" (Heleman 10:4–5). Again to Moses he said, "Blessed art thou, Moses, for I, the Almighty, have chosen thee, and thou shalt be made stronger than many waters; for they shall obey thy command as if thou wert God" (Moses 1:25).

In his final conference address, Elder Bruce R. McConkie made this statement: "If we are to have faith like Enoch and Elijah we must believe what they believed, know what they knew, and live as they lived."[2] In so saying he was echoing what he had heard his own father, Oscar W. McConkie, teach in a general conference address given a third of a century earlier. He said, "The voice of the Spirit spoke to my spirit, for I had asked God to give me faith like unto Enoch and Elijah, because I felt that I must have that kind of faith to accomplish the purpose I was required to seek to accomplish. And the voice of the Spirit said to me: *'Enoch and Elijah obtained their faith through righteousness.'*

"Ah! there is a challenge to every man [and woman] in this Church to have faith through righteousness. There is no other means of obtaining it, and we may pray until our voices fade away, but if we do not have righteousness in our daily lives, we will never have enough faith to win salvation."[3]

In instructing his family, Oscar W. McConkie said, "I never indulged in the deceitful hope that I could win God's favor while I, at the same time, I opposed him in any particular."[4]

THE PRINCIPLE OF RESPONSIBILITY

Leaving a class in which I dispelled the notion that God's love is unconditional, I overheard one student tell another that he liked knowing that God's favor is not unconditional because that placed the responsibility for their relationship with him. It means," he said, "that I can do something about it." I thought that a mature observation on his part. He had discovered the truth that any principle that increases personal responsibility also increases our power to act in righteousness. Such understanding increases our agency.

When I began graduate school, I had visions of sitting at the feet of master teachers who, like the angel in Nephi's dream, would unlock the visions of eternity before me. Needless to say, graduate school was a disappointment—until I came to realize that I was responsible for what I learned, not my teachers. After that it became a very rewarding experience.

When I was offered my present position on the faculty of

Brigham Young University, I was told that "it was the best place in the world to rot and stink." I fully understood what that expression meant. College professors are expected to research, to write, to add in some way to the body of knowledge and enrich what they are teaching. This in turn requires the university to give them considerable freedom. Some, I suppose, may have taken freedom as the license to "rot and stink," but most use it for the purpose for which it was given, and they have a marvelous experience in both learning and teaching.

Such is the pattern of life. Perhaps before we left our first estate someone said to us, "You will be granted great freedom in mortality. You can use it to rot and stink, or you can use it to further your efforts to become as God is, but you cannot become as God is unless you have the freedom to do quite the opposite."

There are no gospel principles—properly understood—that do not increase our personal responsibility. This, as we have already noted, is the flaw in the notion that salvation is by grace alone. There is no question that without Christ we cannot be saved. It is equally true that without our birth as the spirit children of his Father, we would not know life itself. Salvation comes to us by the grace of both the Father and the Son. Yet, as birth into this life was conditional on our acceptance of Christ and our willingness to march under the direction of Michael the Archangel, who led the host of the faithful in casting Satan out of heaven, so it is conditional in this life on our continued faithfulness in advocating the same cause.

There is no freedom from responsibility to be found in the gospel of Jesus Christ. Indeed, it is quite the opposite. As God held Adam responsible for Eve's eating of the forbidden fruit—for they were one—so he holds all parents responsible to teach the principles of the gospel to their children. We are called to positions of responsibility in the Church or the extended family of God to aid and teach one another, and again we are wholly responsible for how and what we teach. Even outside the bounds of the Church, "We believe that governments were instituted of God for the benefit of man; and that he holds men accountable for their acts in relation to them, both in making laws and administering them, for the good and safety of society" (D&C 134:1).

There are no blessings without the attendant responsibility. "For of him unto whom much is given much is required; and he who sins against the greater light shall receive the greater condemnation" (D&C 82:3). Perhaps that is why our revelation says that the Lord gave Joseph Smith "commandments which inspired him" (D&C 20:7). Surely the idea of finding inspiration in receiving more commandments would not appeal to the natural man. Only someone eager to advance in the realm of spiritual things would find inspiration in such a thing. If, however, the definition of agency is the power to act in righteousness, then it would naturally follow that we would increase in agency as we increase in understanding and in righteousness. The more we know, the more we can act upon; and the closer we can live to the Lord's standard, the greater is our association to the powers of heaven.

AGENCY AND CONDEMNATION

In one of the great revelations of this dispensation, the Lord said, "Here is the agency of man, and here is the condemnation of man; because that which was from the beginning is plainly manifest unto them, and they receive not the light. And every man whose spirit receiveth not the light is under condemnation" (D&C 93:31–32). That is, the truths of salvation were revealed to us "in the beginning," in our premortal life. When those same truths are revealed to us anew, we are expected to recognize and embrace them. The power or agency to do so is ours. In doing so we will be blessed; the failure to do so can bring only condemnation.

No blessings accrue from knowingly rejecting divine truths. "It is a philosophical impossibility to reject truth without accepting error," stated Elder Bruce R. McConkie, "to depart from true teachers without cleaving to false ones, to reject the Lord's ministers without giving allegiance to those who follow the other Master."[5] A returned missionary who has wandered from the path of truth and virtue expressed indignation in correspondence with me for what she saw as my intolerance and the supposition that I was right. She argued that we could both be right. She has sought peace of mind in the idea that the true God is nonjudgmental, that he accepts her as she is, and that as Latter-day Saints we have no business pounding the idea into people that there is but one path and that it is both straight and narrow. The difficulty with her reasoning is that she does not want to admit there is such a thing as darkness. To concede the reality of darkness brings with it the possibility that she is in the dark, that she has done wrong, and that she needs to repent. Her arguments are couched to avoid the possibility of such a thing.

We have all heard this kind of argument before. The lines are old, trite, and worn. We are forever brought back to the simple verity that if there is light, there must also be darkness, and to reject the light always brings darkness in its stead.

The apostle Paul spoke of the "deceivableness of unrighteousness in them that perish; because they receive not the love of the truth, that they might be saved. And for this cause God shall send them strong delusion, that they should believe a lie; that they all might be damned who believed not the truth, but had pleasure in unrighteousness" (2 Thessalonians

2:10–12). All missionaries have experienced this. They have had investigators who "desire to know the truth in part, but not all, for they are not right before [the Lord] and must needs repent" (D&C 49:2). They deny the truth to spare themselves the need to repent. In rejecting the light they accept darkness and thus become susceptible to any spiritual disease or counterfeit that comes blowing through the neighborhood.

In Doctrine and Covenants 93 the Lord tells us that the "wicked one cometh and taketh away light and truth, through disobedience, from the children of men, and because of the tradition of their fathers" (D&C 93:39).

GRATITUDE FOR THE GIFT OF GOD

I know of no greater doctrinal evidence of the reality of the God of heaven than the gift of agency. It is the perfect evidence that God is all that we believe him to be: a loving Father willing to share all that he is and has with his children. The only limits on what God will do for us are those that we choose to place on ourselves. Joseph Smith stated the principle thus: "As the Son partakes of the fullness of the Father through the Spirit, so the saints are, by the same Spirit, to be partakers of the same fullness, to enjoy the same glory; for as the Father and the Son are one, so, in like manner, the saints are to be one in them. Through the love of the Father, the mediation of

Jesus Christ, and the gift of the Holy Spirit, they are to be heirs of God, and joint heirs with Jesus Christ."[6] The whole system and plan of salvation exists so that we might become equal with God "in power, and in might, and in dominion" (D&C 76:95), or, as it is stated by Christ in the oath and covenant of the priesthood, "all that my Father hath shall be given unto him" (D&C 84:38).

Agency is the soil in which all other gospel principles grow. Without it they cannot bring forth good fruit. In so saying, I do not suggest that the paramount principle of salvation is anything other than the atonement of Christ. I would, however, suggest that we consider the Grand Council of Heaven, where the very choice of the Savior himself became an expression of the right of choice. In responding as he did to the Father's call, "Whom shall I send?" the premortal Christ was making a freewill offering and thus becoming an agent unto himself.

Nothing in the gospel can be less than a freewill offering. Nor can it be overlooked that when Lucifer was not chosen to become God's Only Begotten Son, he rebelled and sought to destroy the agency of men. Lucifer knew that by destroying their agency, he would also destroy the need for the redemption of Christ. Having failed in that effort in premortality, he now seeks to destroy men by getting them to use their agency unwisely. For this reason the Book of Mormon concludes with the invitation for all to "come unto Christ, and lay hold upon every good gift," with the attendant injunction that they "touch not the evil gift, nor the unclean thing" (Moroni 10:30). Evidencing that our responsibility to do so is both individual and communal, Moroni cites the words of Isaiah: "And awake, and arise from the dust, O Jerusalem; yea, and *put on thy beautiful garments*, O daughter of Zion; and strengthen thy stakes and enlarge thy borders forever, and thou mayest no more be confounded, *that the covenants of the Eternal Father which he hath made unto thee, O house of Israel, may be fulfilled*" (Moroni 10:31; emphasis added; see also Isaiah 52:1). So it is that the Lord has chosen to endow his covenant people with power to bless one another and themselves in the process (D&C 113:8).

Every right choice gives birth to its own blessings. Right choices are as oil to the lamp, or, as holy writ declares, "That which is of God is light; and he that receiveth light, and continueth in God, receiveth more light; and that light growth brighter and brighter until the perfect day" (D&C 50:24). As we advance from grace to grace, we increase in wisdom, understanding, and power of action. Thus, our agency gives purpose and meaning to every choice and action we make. It makes them ours. Agency is as inseparable to life as the Atonement is to the Resurrection. It is a most magnificent gift of God. Well might we ask, then, "For what doth it profit a man if a gift is bestowed upon him, and he receive not the gift? Behold, he rejoices not in that which is given unto him, neither rejoices in him who is the giver of the gift" (D&C 88:33).

My announcement to my father that I wanted to exercise my agency to stay home from church did indeed suggest that I did not understand the principle of agency. His efforts to teach me discipline and responsibility were intended to help me grow up into an understanding of that principle. I have come to realize that in the way we choose to use this divine gift, God gets a perfect measure of our spiritual stature while we at the same time are given the opportunity to express the extent of our interest in residing in his presence. Agency is a sacred trust, a gift from God, an endowment of power that gives life and meaning to all that we do.

NOTES

INTRODUCTION

1 Marion G. Romney, Conference Report, October 1968, 64.

2. Ibid., 65.

3. Thomas Paine, in Norman Cousins, *In God We Trust: The Religious Beliefs and Ideas of the American Founding Fathers* (New York: Harper & Brothers, 1958), 396.

4. Thomas Jefferson, in Cousins, *In God We Trust,* 156.

5. Thomas Jefferson, in Cousins, *In God We Trust,* 162.

Chapter One
AGENCY AND CHOICE

1. *Noah Webster's First Edition of An American Dictionary of the English Language* (1828; facsimile edition, Anaheim, Calif.: Foundation for American Christian Education, 1967), s.v. "agency," "agent."

2. John Ayto, *Dictionary of Word Origins* (New York: Arcade Publishing, 1990), 12.

3. Dallin H. Oaks, "Free Agency and Freedom," in *The Book of Mormon: Second Nephi, the Doctrinal Structure,* edited by Monte S. Nyman and Charles D. Tate Jr. (Provo, Utah: Brigham Young University, Religious Studies Center, 1989), 11.

4. Spencer W. Kimball, *Miracle of Forgiveness* (Salt Lake City, Utah: Bookcraft, 1969), 117; see also Alma 34:35; Helaman 13:38.

5. John A. Widtsoe, "Lesson Course," *Utah Genealogical and Historical Magazine* 25, no. 4 (October 1934): 189.

6. Joseph Fielding Smith, Conference Report, April 1967, 120–21.

7. Boyd K. Packer, "Our Moral Environment," *Ensign,* May 1992, 66–68.

8. Bruce R. McConkie, "The Salvation of Little Children," *Ensign,* April 1977, 6.

9. Lorenzo Snow, *Deseret News Weekly,* 12 May 1894, 637.

10. Richard G. Scott, "Do What Is Right," in *Brigham Young University 1995–96 Speeches* (Provo, Utah: Brigham Young University, 1996), 167–74.

11. S. Dilworth Young, *The Promptings of the Spirit,* Brigham Young University Speeches of the Year (Provo, Utah, 28 October 1959), 3.

Chapter Two
LIBERTY OR LICENSE? THE TESTIMONY OF HISTORY

Aleksandr I. Solzhenitsyn, "A World Split Apart," in *Solzhenitsyn at Harvard,* edited by Ronal Berman (Washington, D.C.: Ethics and Public Policy Center, 1980), 17.

1. Harry S. Stout, "Word and Order in Colonial New England," in *The Bible in America,* edited by Nathan O. Hatch and Mark A. Noll (New York: Oxford University Press, 1982), 29; emphasis added; quoted in Ryan S. Gardner, "A History of the Concepts of Zion and New Jerusalem in America from Early Colonialism to 1835 with a Comparison to the Teachings of the Prophet Joseph Smith" (master's thesis, Brigham Young University, 2002), 37.

2. John Winthrop, "On Liberty," retrieved 2003 from http://www. constitution. org/bcp/winthlib.htm.

3. Ibid.

4. John Winthrop, "A Model of Christian Charity," retrieved 2003 http://www.nv.cc.va.us/home/nvsageh/His121/Part1/winthrop.htm.

5. *The Adams-Jefferson Letters,* ed. Lester J. Cappon (Chapel Hill, N.C.: University of North Carolina Press, 1987), 339–40; emphasis in original; spelling modernized.

6. Barry Alan Shain, *The Myth of American Individualism* (Princeton, N.J.: Princeton University Press, 1994), 197.

7. H. Richard Niebuhr, "Protestant Movement and Democracy," quoted in Shain, *Myth of American Individualism*, 201.

8. Stephen Johnson, 1766, quoted in Shain, *Myth of American Individualism*, 200.

9. Samuel West, "Right to Rebel against Governors," 1776, quoted in Shain, *Myth of American Individualism*, 202.

10. Richard Price, "Observations on the Nature of Liberty," 1776, quoted in Shain, *Myth of American Individualism*, 202.

11. John Zubly, *Law of Liberty,* 1775, quoted in Shain, *Myth of American Individualism*, 203.

12. James Wilson, "Introduction to Law," quoted in Shain, *Myth of American Individualism*, 203.

13. John Mellen, *Great and Happy Doctrine of Liberty,* 1795, quoted in Shain, *Myth of American Individualism*, 208; emphasis in original.

14. Peter Powers, *Jesus Christ the True King,* 1778, quoted in Shain, *Myth of American Individualism*, 222; emphasis added.

15. Shain, *Myth of American Individualism,* 201.

16. Ibid., 204.

17. Ibid., 205.

18. "Faith of Our Forefathers: Religions and the Founding of the American Republic," *Library of Congress Information Bulletin* 57, no. 5 (May 1998); retrieved 2003 from http://www.loc.gov/loc/lcib/9805/religion.html.

19. John Adams, "Proclamation, March 6, 1799," in *A Compilation of the Messages and Papers of the Presidents,* 20 vols. (New York: Bureau of National Literature, 1897), 1:275–76.

20. RJ&L Religious Institutions Group, introduction to "Proclamation: Fasting, Prayer, and Thanksgiving" by John Adams, March 23, 1798;

retrieved 2003 from http://www.churchstatelaw.com/historical materials/8_6_2_3.asp.

21. John Adams, "Proclamation, March 23, 1798," in *Compilation of the Messages and Papers of the Presidents,* 1:259, as cited at http://www.churchstatelaw. com/historicalmaterials/8_6_2_3.asp.

22. Benjamin Franklin, quoted in Eric Foner, *The Story of American Freedom* (New York: W. W. Norton, 1998), 8.

23. Solzhenitsyn, "World Split Apart," 17; emphasis added.

24. Shain, *Myth of American Individualism,* 93; emphasis added.

25. Ibid., 195.

26. Ibid., 206.

Chapter Three
POLITICAL AND RELIGIOUS FREEDOM

James Madison, letter, 1803, quoted in James A. Haught, *2000 Years of Disbelief: Famous People with the Courage to Doubt* (Amherst, N.Y.: Prometheus Books, 1996), 98.

1. Declaration of Independence.

2. Ibid.

3. Marion G. Romney, Conference Report, October 1968, 64.

4. Kenneth D. Wells, *Inner Man and Outer Space,* Brigham Young University Speeches of the Year (Provo, Utah, 30 April 1962), 10.

5. Robert Leckie, *George Washington's War: The Saga of the American Revolution* (New York: HarperPerennial, 1992), 442.

6. Thomas Jefferson, *Autobiography,* 1821, in *The Writings of Thomas Jefferson,* ed. Andrew A. Lipscomb and Albert Ellery Bergh, Monticello ed., 20 vols. (Washington, D. C.: Thomas Jefferson Memorial Association, 1904–5), 1:57.

7. Edwin S. Gaustad, *Sworn on the Altar of God: A Religious Biography of Thomas Jefferson* (Grand Rapids, Mich.: Eerdmans, 1996), 72–73.

8. Edwin S. Gaustad, *Church and State in America* (New York: Oxford University Press, 1999), 39.

9. Gaustad, *Sworn on the Altar of God,* 72.

10. James Madison, quoted in Gaustad, *Church and State in America,* 39.

11. James Madison, quoted in Gaustad, *Church and State in America,* 31.

12. Gaustad, *Sworn on the Altar of God,* 57.

13. Thomas Jefferson, *Statute for Establishing Religious Freedom in the State of Virginia,* retrieved 2003 from http://religiousfreedom.lib.virginia. edu/sacred/vaact.html

Chapter Four
PREREQUISITES FOR AGENCY

Thomas Jefferson to Benjamin Rush, September 23, 1800, quoted in *Writings: Thomas Jefferson,* ed. Merrill D. Peterson (New York: Literary Classics, Viking Press, 1984), 1082.

1. Bruce R. McConkie, *Mormon Doctrine,* 2d ed. (Salt Lake City, Utah: Bookcraft, 1966), 26.
2. William Manchester, *A World Lit Only by Fire: The Medieval Mind and the Renaissance* (Boston: Little, Brown and Company, 1992), 7.
3. Ibid., 35; emphasis in original.
4. Ibid., 59.
5. Robert Williams, quoted in Perry Miller, *Roger Williams: His Contribution to the American Tradition* (New York: Atheneum, 1970), 131.
6. Thomas Jefferson, *Notes on the State of Virginia,* ed. William Peden (Chapel Hill, N.C.: Institute of Early American History and Culture at Williamsburg, Virginia, 1982), 160.
7. Edwin S. Gaustad, *Faith of Our Fathers: Religion and the New Nation* (San Francisco: Harper & Row, 1987), 35.
8. Ibid., 6.
9. Ibid., 98.
10. James Madison to Edward Livingston, July 10, 1822, in *The Writings of James Madison,* ed. Gaillard Hunt, 9 vols. (New York: Putnam's Sons, 1900–1910), 9:98; spelling standardized.

Chapter Five
AGENT OR INSTRUMENT?

Brigham Young, *Journal of Discourses,* 26 vols. (London: Latter-day Saints' Book Depot, 1854–86), 3:205.

1. Bruce R. McConkie, "Agency or Inspiration: Which?" *Speeches of the Year, 1972–73* (Provo: Brigham Young University, 1973), 16.

2. See Brigham Young, *Journal of Discourses,* 26 vols. (London: Latter-day Saints' Book Depot, 1854–86), 3:205.

3. Joseph Smith, *Teachings of the Prophet Joseph Smith,* selected by Joseph Fielding Smith (Salt Lake City: Deseret Book, 1976), 149.

4. Joseph Smith, quoted by John Taylor, *Journal of Discourses,* 10:57–58.

Chapter Six
ENEMIES OF AGENCY

1. George A. Smith, *Journal of Discourses,* 26 vols. (London: Latter-day Saints' Book Depot, 1854–86), 2:330–31.

2. Marion G. Romney, Conference Report, October 1968, 68.

Chapter Seven
AGENCY AND THE LAW OF CONSEQUENCES

1. Robert S. Wood, "On the Responsible Self," *Ensign,* March 2002, 28.

2. Marion G. Romney, Conference Report, October 1968, 65.

3. Fyodor Dostoyevsky, *The Brothers Karamazov,* trans. Constance Garnett, ed. Manuel Komroff (New York: Penguin Books, Signet Classic, 1957, 1980), 245–57.

Chapter Eight
AGENCY AND ITS SEASONS

1. Boyd K. Packer, "Spiritual Crocodiles," *Ensign,* May 1976, 32; emphasis in original.

Chapter Nine
THE GIFT OF GOD

1. Marion G. Romney, Conference Report, October 1968, 65.

2. Bruce R. McConkie, Conference Report, April 1985, 11.

3. Oscar W. McConkie, Conference Report, October 1952, 56–57.

4. Family records in possession of the author.

5. Bruce R. McConkie, *The Promised Messiah* (Salt Lake City: Deseret Book, 1978), 37.

6. Joseph Smith, *Lectures on Faith,* comp. N. B. Lundwall (Salt Lake City: Deseret Book, 1985), 5:3.

INDEX